From our Kitchen to Yours

Our Best Breakfast & Brunch Recipes

Simple recipes for eggs, burritos, hashbrowns, pancakes & more!

*To everyone who
loves breakfast food
any time of day!*

Gooseberry Patch
An imprint of Globe Pequot
246 Goose Lane
Guilford, CT 06437

www.gooseberrypatch.com
1 800 854 6673

Copyright 2019, Gooseberry Patch
978-1-62093-353-4

....

Do you have a tried & true recipe...
tip, craft or memory that you'd like to
see featured in a **Gooseberry Patch**
cookbook? Visit our website at
www.gooseberrypatch.com and
follow the easy steps to submit
your favorite family recipe.

Or send them to us at:
Gooseberry Patch
PO Box 812
Columbus, OH 43216-0812

Don't forget to include the number
of servings your recipe makes, plus
your name, address, phone number
and email address. If we select your
recipe, your name will appear right
along with it... and you'll receive a
FREE copy of the book!

CONTENTS

Easy-to-make
breakfast recipes

∷∷∷∷∷∷∷∷∷∷∷∷

∷∷∷∷∷∷∷∷∷∷∷∷

Our Best Breakfast & Brunch Recipes

Rise & shine! Do you love a a hearty breakfast first thing in the morning, or would you rather start with a muffin and coffee at 9:00am? These days, there's no wrong answer! To help you jump start every day of the week, we've gathered our favorite egg dishes, pancakes and waffles, muffins, coffee cakes and even a few surprises.

Here are a few ideas to get you started. If you're looking for...

Grab & Go Recipes, try:
- Smoothies - filled with fresh ingredients, these are just the thing to fill you up
- Make-ahead breakfast burritos and sandwiches - big-batch cooking saves you time during the week
- Sweet or savory oatmeal - spoon this into a to-go container and pop it in your lunchbox
- Yogurt parfaits - layer this in a pretty jelly jar the night before, grab it on your way out the door

Lazy-Day Weekend Recipes, try:
- Pancakes, waffles and French toast - need we say more?
- Steak & eggs - the best dinner for breakfast meal ever invented
- Egg-topped burgers - have you tried one yet? We think you'll love them as much as we do!

Breakfast & Brunch Buffet Ideas, try:
- Crowd-pleasing casseroles - hearty and easy to feed a brunch bunch
- Satisfying sides - lots of choices from hash to hashbrowns, breakfast meats and sausage gravy
- Customizable dishes - omelets, frittatas and breakfast tacos are perfect here
- Coffee cakes and pastries - everyone likes a little bite of sweetness at breakfast

Mid-Morning Snacks, try:

- Sweet breads - a thick slice of banana bread topped with almond butter will hold you 'til noon!
- Muffins - a fruit-filled muffin and a slice of cheese makes a great coffee break
- Granola - eaten straight from a container or with a cup of milk, it's a sweet pick-me-up

Remember, anything goes for breakfast...so mix it up a bit and have fun!

Veggie & Sprouts Bagel, Page 14

CHAPTER ONE

Grab & Go

Bowl-Free Cereal-to-Go, Page 36

Krista's Breakfast Tacos, Page 20

Melissa Bordenkircher, Columbus, OH

Tropical Smoothies

A chilled, fruity smoothie really hits the spot on a summer's day.

Makes 2 servings

1 c. mango, peeled, pitted and cubed
3/4 c. banana, sliced
2/3 c. milk
1 t. honey
1/4 t. vanilla extract
Optional: 1 T. powdered milk

Arrange mango in a single layer on a baking sheet; freeze for one hour. Place frozen mango and remaining ingredients in a blender. Process until smooth. Pour into glasses to serve.

Elizabeth Quigley, League City, TX

Sugar-Free Granola

I've been cutting sugar from my diet due to health issues, but I wanted something sweet to sprinkle on top of my yogurt. So I created this granola... it is so yummy!

Makes 8 servings

2 c. rolled oats, uncooked
1/2 c. raw walnuts or other nuts, chopped
1 t. orange zest
1 t. sea salt
1/3 c. sugar-free maple syrup
1/4 c. canola oil

In a bowl, combine oats, nuts, orange zest and salt; mix well. Combine syrup and oil in a separate bowl. Pour over oat mixture; mix well. Spoon mixture onto a parchment paper-lined baking sheet. Bake at 325 degrees for 30 minutes, stirring every 10 minutes. Remove from oven; allow to cool. Store in an airtight container.

★ SIMPLE INGREDIENT SWAP ★
Try this easy fruit smoothie on a hot summer morning...just substitute milk for water in a favorite frozen fruit juice. Pour into the blender with several ice cubes and blend until frothy. So refreshing!

Tropical Smoothies

Jo Ann, Gooseberry Patch

Good Morning Blueberry Shake

I enjoy a yummy breakfast shake...
this drink blends up fast and is
so pretty!

Makes 4 servings

2-1/2 c. blueberries
1-1/4 c. apple juice
1 c. frozen vanilla yogurt
1/4 c. milk
3/4 t. cinnamon
Garnish: additional blueberries

Combine all ingredients except
garnish in a blender and process until
smooth. Garnish with additional
blueberries. Serve immediately.

Mary Ann Lewis, Olive Branch, MS

Best-Ever Breakfast Bars

Toss in a few chocolate chips just
for fun!

Serves 8 to 12

1 c. granola
1 c. quick-cooking oats, uncooked
1 c. nuts, coarsely chopped
1/2 c. all-purpose flour
1/4 c. brown sugar, packed
1/8 t. cinnamon
1/2 c. dried fruit, chopped into small
    pieces
2 T. ground whole flax seed meal
1/3 c. canola oil
1/3 c. honey
1/2 t. vanilla extract
1 egg, beaten

Combine granola, oats, nuts, flour,
sugar, cinnamon, dried fruit and
flax seed meal in a large bowl. Whisk
together oil, honey and vanilla; stir
into granola mixture. Add egg; stir
to blend. Press mixture into a
parchment paper-lined 8"x8" baking
pan. Bake at 325 degrees for 30 to
35 minutes, until lightly golden
around edges. Remove from oven
and cool 30 minutes to one hour.
Slice into bars.

Good Morning Blueberry Shake

Kristi Likes, Stonington, IL

Ham Quiche Cups

On busy mornings, it's so handy to have some of these little gems tucked in the freezer, ready to reheat. They're very easy to change up by using sausage instead of ham and adding your favorite cheese.

Makes one dozen muffins

1 T. butter
1 c. frozen diced onion and peppers
   seasoning blend
4 slices cooked deli ham, chopped
6 eggs, beaten
1/2 t. Italian seasoning
pepper to taste
1 c. shredded mozzarella cheese

Melt butter in a skillet over medium heat. Add onion blend and cook until vegetables are tender, about 4 minutes. Add ham and cook another minute. Remove skillet from stove; let stand for 5 to 10 minutes. Meanwhile, preheat oven to 350 degrees. In a bowl, whisk together eggs and seasonings; mix in cheese. Add onion mixture and stir until combined. Ladle into 12 greased muffin cups, 2 tablespoons per cup. Bake at 350 degrees for about 20 minutes, until eggs are set. Serve immediately, or wrap individually and place in plastic zipping bags. May keep refrigerated up to 2 days or frozen for one month. Warm in microwave.

★ FREEZE IT ★ **When cheese is on sale, go ahead and stock up! Pop it into the freezer to use later. Cheese tends to turn crumbly when frozen... not so good in recipes using fresh cheese, but perfectly yummy in these Ham Quiche Cups and baked casserole dishes. To use, let cheese thaw overnight in the refrigerator.**

Ham Quiche Cups

Jennifer Hollingsworth,
Powder Springs, GA

Veggie & Sprouts Bagel

I made this for myself and was amazed at how much I loved it! When my kids saw how much I liked it, they took what I had left and begged me to make more. It's such a fresh-tasting and healthy snack.

Makes one serving

1 mini whole-wheat bagel, halved
   and lightly toasted
1 T. onion & chive flavored cream
   cheese, softened
2 T. alfalfa sprouts
2 slices tomato
2 to 4 cucumber slices
sea salt to taste

Spread each bagel half with cream cheese. Top each half with alfalfa sprouts, one tomato slice and one to 2 cucumber slices. Sprinkle with just a little salt to taste.

Jen Thomas, Santa Rosa, CA

French Toast Pick-Up Sticks

Our kids love this French toast they can eat with their hands! Save time by making ahead and freezing. Pop in the toaster to serve.

Makes 2 to 4 servings

2 eggs, beaten
3/4 c. milk
1 t. vanilla extract
4 slices bread, each cut into 4 strips
1 T. butter
Garnish: maple syrup, favorite
   preserves

Whisk together eggs, milk and vanilla in a shallow bowl. Dip bread strips, soaking well. Melt butter in a skillet over medium heat. Add bread strips; cook until golden on both sides. Serve warm with syrup or preserves for dipping.

★ SAVVY SECRET ★ **Whip up tasty maple butter in no time! Delicious on French Toast Pick-Up Sticks, pancakes and waffles. Just combine 1/2 cup butter with 3/4 cup maple syrup.**

Veggie & Sprouts Bagel

Gladys Kielar, Whitehouse, OH

Breakfast Milkshake

Children love this fruit-filled shake.

Makes 2 servings

2 ripe bananas, sliced into 1-inch
   chunks
1/4 c. blueberries
5 to 10 whole strawberries,
   quartered and hulled
1/2 c. milk

Combine fruits in a plastic freezer
bag; seal and freeze for 3 hours to
overnight. Place the frozen fruits in
a blender or food processor. If fruits
are rock-hard, let them thaw a little.
Add milk and process until smooth
and thick. Pour into mugs and serve
with spoons.

Cheri Maxwell, Gulf Breeze, FL

Break-of-Day Smoothie

Make this just the way you like it,
using your favorite flavors of yogurt
and fruit.

Makes 2 servings

15-1/4 oz. can fruit cocktail
8-oz. container vanilla yogurt
1 c. pineapple juice
6 to 8 ice cubes
Optional: 3 to 4 T. wheat germ

Combine all ingredients in a blender.
Blend until smooth.

★ SAVVY SECRET ★ Sprinkle wheat
germ or ground flax seed into smoothies
and baked goods for extra fiber and a
nutty taste.

Breakfast Milkshake

Vickie, Gooseberry Patch

Cheddar & Bacon Breakfast Sandwiches

Substitute Monterey Jack or Swiss cheese for a variety of flavor!

Makes 4 servings

3 eggs, beaten
1/4 c. milk
2 T. butter
8 thick slices bread
12 slices Cheddar cheese
1/2 T. chopped walnuts
4 slices bacon, crisply cooked and
   crumbled

In a large bowl, whisk together eggs and milk; set aside. Prepare a griddle or large skillet by melting butter over low heat. Dip only one side of 4 bread slices in egg mixture. Place 4 bread slices, coated side down, on griddle or in skillet. Top each bread slice with 3 cheese slices. Sprinkle cheese with an equal amount of walnuts and bacon. Dip only one side of the remaining 4 bread slices in egg mixture and place over walnuts and bacon, coated side up. Cook 5 minutes per side, or until bread is golden and cheese is melted.

Joyceann Dreibelbis, Wooster, OH

Scrambled Egg Wrap

You'll never be tempted to skip breakfast again after trying this tasty breakfast treat! It takes just 10 minutes to make one serving and is so easy to double or triple. Enjoy!

Makes one serving

2 eggs, lightly beaten
1 whole-wheat flour tortilla
2 T. herb-flavored cream cheese,
   softened
2 T. shredded Cheddar cheese
1-1/2 t. fresh basil, chopped
1-1/2 t. fresh chives, chopped
1 T. salsa

Coat a small skillet with non-stick vegetable spray; heat over medium-low heat. Add eggs and cook for 2 minutes, stirring constantly. Spread tortilla with cream cheese; top with eggs and remaining ingredients. Roll up tortilla, folding in sides; place on an ungreased baking sheet. Bake at 300 degrees for 3 minutes, or until warmed through.

Cheddar & Bacon Breakfast Sandwiches

Krista Marshall, Fort Wayne, IN

Krista's Breakfast Tacos

I created these fun and tasty tacos for breakfast or brunch when I discovered taco-size tortillas are easier for my son Alex to handle than the large burrito-size ones.

Makes 8 tacos

1 lb. mild or hot ground pork
  breakfast sausage
1 green pepper, finely chopped
3 to 4 tomatoes, chopped and
  divided
8 eggs, beaten
2 T. whipping cream
1 c. shredded taco-blend cheese,
  divided
salt and pepper to taste
8 taco-size flour tortillas
Optional: sliced avocado

In a large skillet over medium heat, brown sausage until no longer pink. Drain sausage and remove to a bowl, reserving one tablespoon drippings; set aside. In same skillet, sauté green pepper and half of tomatoes in reserved drippings until tender. In a large bowl, whisk eggs, cream, 1/3 cup cheese, salt and pepper. When pepper mixture is tender, reduce heat to low; add egg mixture and sausage. Cook over low heat, stirring constantly, until eggs are scrambled and cooked through, about 10 minutes. Fill tortillas with egg mixture. Top with remaining tomatoes, cheese and avocado, if desired.

★ PENNY PINCHER ★ A dollar-store package of paper coffee filters is oh-so handy in the kitchen. Perfect for on-the-go taco holders at breakfast!

Krista's Breakfast Tacos

Terri Scungio, Williamsburg, VA

Country Ham Biscuits

I usually make these biscuits with sausage, but recently I tried country ham instead...everyone loved them!

Makes 2 to 3 dozen

2 c. self-rising flour
1/2 c. plus 3 T. butter, divided
1 c. cooked ham, ground
1-1/2 c. shredded sharp Cheddar
   cheese
3/4 c. plus 2 T. buttermilk

Add flour to a bowl. Cut in 1/2 cup butter with a pastry cutter or fork until mixture resembles coarse crumbs. Stir in ham and cheese. Add buttermilk; stir with fork until a moist dough forms. Drop dough by heaping teaspoonfuls onto a lightly greased baking sheet. Bake at 450 degrees for 10 to 13 minutes, until lightly golden. Melt remaining butter and brush over hot biscuits.

Shelly Turner, Boise, ID

Steak & Egg Breakfast Burrito

Such a great way to enjoy classic steak and eggs when you're in a hurry!

Makes 2 servings

2 frozen sliced sandwich steaks
4 eggs
2 T. milk
2 t. fresh chives, chopped
salt and pepper to taste
2 corn tortillas
salsa to taste
1/2 c. shredded Mexican-blend
   cheese, divided

In a skillet over medium heat, cook steaks until no longer pink; drain and set aside. Beat together eggs, milk, chives, salt and pepper. In same skillet, scramble eggs to desired doneness. Divide eggs evenly between tortillas; top each with steak, salsa and cheese. Roll up and microwave on high setting for 20 to 30 seconds to melt cheese.

★ HOT TIP ★ Tortillas come in several different sizes and types... you may even be able to find sopes, which are small thick corn disks with a raised edge. Here's a handy size guide: for tacos, use 6-inch tortillas; for fajitas, use 8-inch tortillas; for burritos, use 10-inch tortillas.

Country Ham Biscuits

Penny Sherman, Cumming, GA

Grab & Go Breakfast Cookies

These cookies are perfect for those busy mornings when you have to rush out the door.

Makes one to 1-1/2 dozen

1/2 c. butter, softened
1/2 c. sugar
1 egg, beaten
2 T. frozen orange juice concentrate, thawed
1 T. orange zest
1-1/4 c. all-purpose flour
1 t. baking powder
1/2 c. wheat & barley cereal

Blend together butter and sugar in a bowl until light and fluffy. Beat in egg, orange juice and zest; set aside. Combine flour and baking powder in a small bowl; stir into butter mixture until blended. Stir in cereal. Drop by tablespoonfuls, 2 inches apart, on an ungreased baking sheet. Bake at 350 degrees for 10 to 12 minutes, until golden around edges. Cool on a wire rack.

Shirl Parsons, Cape Carteret, NC

Banana-Mango Soy Smoothie

A cool refreshing pick-me-up drink... especially good for those who can't tolerate milk!

Makes 6 servings

2 c. vanilla or plain soy milk
2 to 3 bananas, sliced and frozen
6 mangoes, peeled, pitted, cubed and frozen
1 T. honey, or to taste

Combine all ingredients in a blender. Blend on high setting until smooth and frothy. Pour into tall glasses.

★ FLAVOR BURST ★ Add chopped nuts or sunflower seeds to Grab & Go Breakfast Cookies and morning muffins to add a nice crunch and extra flavor.

Grab & Go Breakfast Cookies

Carolyn Britton, Millry, AL

Sausage Muffins

These are great to make ahead and freeze individually. Just heat and serve for a quick breakfast or snack.

Makes 6 muffins

1 lb. ground turkey sausage
1/4 c. butter
5-oz. jar sharp pasteurized process
   cheese spread
1/4 t. garlic powder
6 English muffins, split

In a skillet over medium heat, brown sausage; drain. Add butter, cheese and garlic powder; mix and cook until cheese melts. Spread sausage mixture on 6 English muffin halves. Place on an ungreased baking sheet and bake at 350 degrees for 15 minutes, or until heated through. Top with remaining halves of English muffins.

★ SKINNY SECRET ★ For extra-lean ground turkey or beef, pour meat into a colander after browning. Rinse with hot water...this washes away most of the remaining fat.

Sausage Muffins

Michelle Case, Yardley, PA

Break-of-Day Berry Parfait

So pretty served in a parfait or champagne glass!

Makes 2 servings

1 c. strawberries, hulled and
　sliced
1/2 c. raspberries
1/4 c. blackberries
1 c. bran & raisin cereal
6-oz. container strawberry
　yogurt

In a bowl, combine berries; divide into 2 small bowls. Top each with cereal. Spoon yogurt over top.

Ellen Gibson, Orlando, FL

Whole-Grain Jam Squares

These look so tempting stacked on a jadite serving plate, and their taste is out of this world.

Makes 2 dozen

2 c. quick-cooking oats, uncooked
1-3/4 c. all-purpose flour
3/4 t. salt
1/2 t. baking soda
1 c. butter, softened
1 c. brown sugar, packed
1/2 c. chopped walnuts
1 t. cinnamon
3/4 to 1 c. strawberry preserves

Combine all ingredients except preserves in a bowl; stir until large crumbs form. Reserve 2 cups oat mixture and set aside. Press remaining mixture into a greased 13"x9" baking pan. Spread preserves over the top; sprinkle with reserved oat mixture. Bake at 400 degrees for 25 to 30 minutes, until golden. Cool; cut into squares.

Break-of-Day Berry Parfait

Courtney Stultz, Columbus, KS

Veggie Egg Muffins

As a busy mom, mornings are crazy for me. I love finding shortcuts anywhere I can and these healthy muffins are perfect. They are loaded with veggies for great nutrition. They freeze well too!

Makes 20 muffins

18 eggs or egg white equivalent, beaten
6-oz. container plain yogurt or 3/4 c. milk
1 t. dried sage
1 t. sea salt
1/2 t. pepper
1 c. broccoli, finely chopped
1/2 c. cauliflower, finely chopped
1/2 c. carrots, peeled and finely chopped
1 to 2 c. shredded Cheddar cheese
Garnish: sour cream, salsa, catsup or sriracha sauce

Combine all ingredients except garnish in a large bowl; whisk until blended. Pour into 20 ungreased muffin cups, filling 2/3 full. Bake at 375 degrees for about 20 to 25 minutes, until eggs are set and golden. Garnish as desired. To freeze, let muffins cool completely. Store in a plastic freezer bag or container for up to 3 months. Reheat in microwave or oven.

★ DOUBLE DUTY ★ Save leftover veggies from dinner to use in Veggie Egg Muffins. Sautéed peppers and onions, diced green beans, chopped tomatoes and steamed spinach would all taste great.

Veggie Egg Muffins

Audrey Lett, Newark, DE

Suzanne's Tomato Melt

Start your day with fresh garden flavor...hearty and delicious!

Makes one serving

1/4 c. shredded Cheddar cheese
1 onion bagel or English muffin, split
2 tomato slices
1 T. shredded Parmesan cheese

Sprinkle half the Cheddar cheese over each bagel or English muffin half. Top with a tomato slice. Sprinkle half the Parmesan cheese over each tomato. Broil about 6 inches from heat for 4 to 5 minutes, until cheese is bubbly.

Lynne McKaige, Savage, MN

Baked Egg Soufflé

Easy and delicious...I hope you'll enjoy this dish as much as we do!

Makes 6 servings

12 slices white bread
2 T. butter, softened
6 slices deli ham
6 slices American cheese
3 c. milk
4 eggs, beaten
salt and pepper to taste

Spread one side of each bread slice with butter. Arrange 6 slices butter-side down in a lightly buttered 13"x9" baking pan. Arrange ham and cheese on top. Cover with remaining bread, butter-side up. Whisk milk and eggs together until frothy; pour over all. Sprinkle with salt and pepper. Bake, uncovered, at 350 degrees for 50 minutes, or until golden. Let stand for 5 minutes before serving.

★ SAVVY SECRET ★ Planning a midday brunch? Along with breakfast foods like Baked Egg Soufflé, coffee cake and cereal, offer a light, savory main dish or two for those who have already enjoyed breakfast.

Suzanne's Tomato Melt

Emily Hartzell, Portland, IN

Honey Crunch Granola

For a delicious, healthy breakfast, serve over vanilla yogurt with fresh berries and bananas!

Makes 8 servings

4 c. long-cooking oats, uncooked
1/2 c. unsalted slivered almonds
1/4 c. unsalted sunflower kernels
1/2 c. honey
1/2 c. butter
2 t. cinnamon
1/8 t. ground cloves
1 t. vanilla extract
1/8 t. salt

Mix oats, almonds and sunflower kernels in a large bowl; set aside. Combine honey, butter, spices, vanilla and salt in a microwave-safe bowl. Microwave on high setting until butter and honey are melted; stir well. Pour honey mixture over oat mixture; toss until well coated. Spread on a lightly greased 15"x10" jelly-roll pan. Bake at 350 degrees for 20 minutes, or until lightly golden. Allow to cool completely; store in an airtight container.

★ TAKE IT TO GO ★ When a free morning with girlfriends means barn & tag sales or flea-market shopping, scoop Honey Crunch Granola into easy-to-tote sports bottles...ideal for breakfast on-the-road.

Honey Crunch Granola

Amanda Pennings, Walla Walla, WA

Bowl-Free Cereal-to-Go

Cereal without the milk! A big handful of this and I'm out the door, ready to start my day.

Serves 12 to 14

1/4 c. sugar
1/2 t. cinnamon
1 c. bite-size crispy corn cereal squares
1 c. bite-size crispy rice cereal squares
1 c. bite-size crispy wheat cereal squares
1 c. honey-nut doughnut-shaped oat cereal
3/4 c. sliced almonds, toasted
1/3 c. butter, melted
1 c. dried banana chips
1/2 c. dried blueberries or raisins

In a small bowl, mix sugar and cinnamon; set aside. In a large, microwave-safe bowl, combine cereals and melted butter; toss until evenly coated. Microwave, uncovered, on high for 2 minutes, stirring after one minute. Stir in sugar mixture and banana chips until evenly coated. Microwave, uncovered, for one additional minute. Spread on wax paper to cool. Transfer to an airtight container; stir in blueberries or raisins.

★ VARIETY FOR FUN ★ Mix and match cereal, nuts and dried fruit for fun and variety in this cereal-to-go recipe. Walnuts, pecans and cashews are good choices. Dried cranberries, cherries and pineapple add lots of flavor too!

Bowl-Free Cereal-to-Go

Dana Cunningham, Lafayette, LA

Dilly Egg Salad Sandwiches

A new twist on an old standby, these are extra cute wrapped in parchment or wax paper and tied with string. Serve with crisp kettle-style potato chips for crunch.

Makes 4 servings

8 eggs, hard-boiled, peeled and
   chopped
1/4 c. mayonnaise
1-1/2 T. Dijon mustard
1/4 c. celery, minced
2 T. green onions, minced
2 T. fresh dill, chopped
2 t. white vinegar
salt and pepper to taste
8 slices country-style bread
2 c. shredded lettuce

Combine all ingredients except bread and lettuce in a bowl; mix well and chill. When ready to serve, divide egg salad evenly among 4 slices of bread; top with lettuce and remaining bread slices. Serve immediately.

★ TAKE IT TO GO ★ Egg salad isn't just a lunchtime favorite...it's perfect for breakfast on the go. Try it on toasted English muffins or bagels!

Dilly Egg Salad Sandwiches

Steak & Egg Hash, Page 70

CHAPTER TWO

Eggs & Breakfast Bowls

Apricot Oat Breakfast, Page 68

Poached Pesto Eggs, Page 50

Nick Jenner, Chicago, IL

Sheet Pan Steak & Eggs

I make breakfast for my golf buddies sometimes before we hit the links. Cooking everything in one pan makes clean-up easy.

Serves 3 to 6

2 T. olive oil
2 lbs. potatoes, peeled and diced
4 cloves garlic, minced
1/4 c. grated Parmesan cheese
1/2 t. salt, divided
1/2 t. pepper, divided
2 lbs. beef sirloin steak, sliced into
    1-inch pieces
3 to 6 eggs
Optional: chopped fresh chives

Spread oil on a large rimmed baking sheet; spread potatoes over oil. Sprinkle with garlic and cheese; toss to combine. Sprinkle with half each of salt and pepper. Bake at 400 degrees for 20 to 25 minutes, until potatoes are golden. Remove pan from oven; preheat oven to broil. Season beef with remaining salt and pepper; add to pan in a single layer. With the back of a spoon, create 3 to 6 wells in potato mixture. Gently crack eggs into wells. Broil until egg whites have set and beef is cooked through. Garnish with chives, if desired.

★ SAVVY SIDE ★ **A fresh brunch side dish... fruit kabobs! Just slide pineapple chunks, apple slices, grapes, orange wedges and strawberries onto a wooden skewer. Easy to make, and no plate required!**

Sheet Pan Steak & Eggs

Staci Meyers, Montezuma, GA

Maple Ham & Eggs Cups

Ham and eggs make such a great breakfast or brunch...the kids will love the novelty too.

Makes 6 servings

1 T. butter, melted
6 slices deli ham
1 T. maple syrup
1 t. butter, cut into 6 pieces
6 eggs
salt and pepper to taste
English muffins, toast or biscuits

Brush muffin cups in pans with melted butter; line each cup with a slice of ham. Pour 1/2 teaspoon maple syrup over each ham slice; top with one pat of butter. Crack one egg into each ham cup; season with salt and pepper as desired. Bake at 400 degrees for 20 minutes, or until eggs are set. Remove muffin cups from oven; use a spoon or gently twist each serving to loosen. Serve on English muffins, with toast or on split biscuits.

Wendy Jacobs, Idaho Falls, ID

Potato & Onion Frittata

Make a hearty, warm breakfast using a little leftover ham and potato from last night's dinner.

Makes 6 servings

2 to 3 T. olive oil, divided
1 yellow onion, thinly sliced
1/4 c. cooked ham, diced
1 c. potatoes, peeled, cooked and
   diced
4 eggs, beaten
1/3 c. shredded Parmesan cheese
salt to taste

Heat 2 tablespoons oil over medium heat in a non-stick skillet. Add onion; cook and stir for 2 to 3 minutes. Add ham and potatoes. Cook until onion and potatoes are lightly golden. With a slotted spoon, remove mixture to a bowl; cool slightly. Stir eggs, cheese and salt into onion mixture. Return skillet to medium heat; add the remaining oil, if needed. When skillet is hot, add onion mixture. Cook until frittata is golden on the bottom and top begins to set, about 4 to 5 minutes. Place a plate over skillet and carefully invert frittata onto the plate. Slide frittata back into skillet. Cook until bottom is lightly golden, 2 to 3 minutes. Cut into wedges; serve warm or at room temperature.

Maple Ham & Eggs Cups

Kathy Grashoff, Fort Wayne, IN

Mary Ann's Sunrise Egg Bake

This is my absolute go-to egg casserole...it is so good! I always make a couple of all-vegetable bakes, too. Try adding onions, colorful red and green peppers and whatever else you like.

Makes 12 servings

1 doz. eggs
1 c. evaporated milk
2 t. dry mustard
salt and pepper to taste
8-oz. pkg. shredded Cheddar cheese
1 c. cooked ham, chopped
8-oz. can sliced mushrooms, drained
1/4 c. butter, diced

Beat together eggs, milk, mustard, salt and pepper in a large bowl. Stir in cheese, ham and mushrooms. Pour into a lightly greased 13"x9" baking pan; dot with butter. Bake, uncovered, at 300 degrees for 45 minutes. Cool slightly before cutting into squares.

Diane Cohen, The Woodlands, TX

Brats, Taters & Apples

The taste combination of bratwurst, potatoes and apples is something special indeed. It may sound strange, but one bite and you'll be a believer.

Makes 6 servings

5 to 6 bratwurst pork sausage links, sliced
5 potatoes, peeled and cubed
27-oz. pkg. sauerkraut, drained and rinsed
1 tart apple, cored and chopped
1 onion, chopped
1/4 c. brown sugar, packed

In a skillet over medium heat, brown bratwurst on all sides. Combine remaining ingredients in a slow cooker. Stir in bratwurst and pan drippings; cover and cook on high setting for 4 to 6 hours, until potatoes and apples are tender.

Mary Ann's Sunrise Egg Bake

Laura Fuller, Fort Wayne, IN

Laura's Eggs Benedict

You can easily substitute split biscuits for the English muffins and even a sausage patty for the Canadian bacon... it's tasty either way.

Makes 8 servings

4 English muffins, split and toasted
16 slices Canadian bacon
8 eggs
1/4 c. plus 1 T. butter, divided
1/4 c. all-purpose flour
1 t. paprika
1/8 t. nutmeg
2 c. milk
8-oz. pkg. shredded Swiss cheese
1/2 c. chicken broth
1 c. corn flake cereal, crushed

Arrange muffins split-side up in a lightly greased 13"x9" baking pan. Place 2 bacon slices on each muffin half. Fill a large skillet halfway with water; bring to just boiling. Break one egg into a dish; carefully slide into water. Repeat with 3 more eggs. Simmer, uncovered, 3 minutes or just until set. Remove eggs with a slotted spoon. Repeat with remaining eggs. Place one egg on each muffin half; set aside. In a saucepan over medium heat, melt 1/4 cup butter; stir in flour, paprika and nutmeg. Add milk; cook and stir until thick and bubbly. Stir in cheese until melted; add broth. Carefully spoon sauce over eggs. Melt remaining butter; stir in cereal and sprinkle over top. Cover and refrigerate overnight. Bake, uncovered, at 375 degrees for 20 to 25 minutes, until heated through.

★ SAVVY SWAP ★ More like ham than bacon, Canadian bacon is a cured, lightly smoked pork loin, adding a slightly smoky flavor to dishes. Don't have any handy? Try bacon, pancetta or thinly sliced ham.

Laura's Eggs Benedict

Terri Carr, Lewes, DE

Poached Pesto Eggs

I'm always looking for new ideas for my husband's breakfast. I thought pesto and eggs would be a good combination. He loved it!

Serves one to 2

2 eggs
2 to 3 T. basil pesto sauce
2 slices bread, toasted
2 to 4 slices tomato
Garnish: fresh parsley, chopped

Add 2 inches water to a skillet. Bring to a simmer over high heat. One egg at a time, break eggs into a cup and slide into simmering water. Cook eggs for 3 to 5 minutes, to desired doneness. Spread pesto over toast slices; top with tomato slices. With a slotted spoon, top each slice with an egg. Sprinkle with parsley.

Melanie Lowe, Dover, DE

Milk & Honey Couscous

This quick-to-fix breakfast is perfect for those chilly mornings when you need something to fill you up and keep you warm.

Makes 6 servings

2 c. milk
2 T. honey
1 T. cinnamon
2 c. couscous, uncooked
1/3 c. dried apricots, chopped
1/3 c. raisins
1/2 c. slivered almonds

Combine milk, honey and cinnamon in a saucepan over medium heat. Bring to a boil; stir in couscous. Remove from heat; cover and let stand for 5 minutes. Fold in remaining ingredients.

★ FLAVOR BURST ★ Try making pesto at home...it's so flavorful! In a food processor, combine one bunch fresh basil, 3 tablespoons pine nuts, 3 cloves garlic and 3/4 cup shredded Parmesan cheese. Drizzle with 3 to 4 tablespoons olive oil; process until puréed.

Poached Pesto Eggs

Stacie Avner, Delaware, OH

Crab, Corn & Pepper Frittata

When it is in season, use fresh corn.

Serves 4 to 6

6 eggs, beaten
1/3 c. corn
1/3 c. mayonnaise
1/4 c. milk
2 T. green onions, chopped
2 T. red pepper, chopped
salt and pepper to taste
1 c. crabmeat, flaked
1 c. shredded Monterey Jack cheese
Garnish: chopped green onions

Whisk together eggs, corn, mayonnaise, milk, onions, red pepper and salt and pepper to taste. Gently stir in crabmeat. Pour into a greased 10" pie plate. Bake at 350 degrees for 15 to 20 minutes. Sprinkle with cheese and bake for 5 more minutes, or until cheese is melted. Garnish with green onions.

Teresa Stopher, Gainesville, TX

Fresh Asparagus Omelet

Every spring, I can't wait for the asparagus to start popping up in my garden so my husband and I can savor this omelet. It's such a treat with warm buttered biscuits and honey!

Serves 2 to 4

1 T. butter
1 T. olive oil
8 stalks asparagus, cut into 1/2-inch pieces
1/4 onion, chopped
6 eggs, beaten
1/4 c. milk
salt and pepper to taste
1/2 c. shredded Swiss cheese

In a non-stick skillet, heat butter and oil over medium heat. Add asparagus and onion; cook for 5 minutes, or until tender. In a bowl, combine eggs, milk, salt and pepper. Beat egg mixture with a fork just until bubbles begin to appear; pour over asparagus mixture. Cook until eggs set on top; lift edges with a spatula to allow uncooked eggs to run under cooked eggs. When eggs are set, top with cheese. Cut into wedges.

Crab, Corn & Pepper Frittata

Betty Bunting, Huber Heights, OH

Baked Sausage & Eggs

I often make this with heat & serve sausages when I want to save a little time.

Makes 6 servings

6 pork breakfast sausage links
2 c. shredded sharp Cheddar cheese
1 T. all-purpose flour
1 c. shredded Monterey Jack cheese
6 eggs, lightly beaten
1/2 c. half-and-half
1 t. Worcestershire sauce

Cook sausage links according to package directions; drain on paper towels. Meanwhile, combine Cheddar cheese and flour; sprinkle evenly in the bottom of an ungreased shallow 1-1/2 quart casserole dish. Sprinkle with Monterey Jack cheese and set aside. In a separate bowl, whisk together eggs, half-and-half and Worcestershire sauce; pour over cheese mixture. Arrange sausages over egg mixture. Cover and chill for 8 hours. Remove from refrigerator. Let stand, covered, at room temperature for 30 minutes. Uncover and bake at 350 degrees for 45 minutes, or until set and lightly golden. Let stand 5 minutes before serving.

★ VARIETY FOR FUN ★ For a brunch buffet, serve an assortment of artisan cheeses. Line a white-washed basket with red and white homespun, tie a red bow on the handle and fill it with a variety of cheeses and crackers. Perfect for guests to nibble on...they may even discover a new favorite or two!

Baked Sausage & Eggs

Donna Jones, Mikado, MI

Spicy Black Bean Scrambled Eggs

Top this with a dollop of sour cream for a delicious breakfast.

Makes one serving

1/4 c. canned black beans, drained
    and rinsed
1/4 c. chunky salsa
1/8 t. chili powder
Optional: 1/8 t. red pepper flakes
2 eggs, beaten
6-inch corn tortilla, warmed
1/4 c. shredded sharp Cheddar
    cheese
Optional: additional salsa

Spray a small skillet with non-stick vegetable spray. Add beans, salsa and desired seasonings; cook over medium heat one minute, stirring frequently. Add eggs; stir to combine. Continue cooking and stirring until eggs are fully cooked. Spoon egg mixture onto tortilla. Top with cheese and additional salsa, if desired. Serve immediately.

Donna Maltman, Toledo, OH

Country Sausage & Apples

A truly delicious slow-cooker recipe. There's just something about the combination of sausage and apples that tastes so good!

Makes 4 servings

1-lb. pkg. smoked pork sausage, sliced
    into 1-inch pieces
3 Granny Smith apples, cored and
    diced
1 c. brown sugar, packed
1/4 to 1/2 c. water

Place sausage in a slow cooker; top with apples. Sprinkle with brown sugar and drizzle water over all. Stir gently; cover and cook on high setting for 1-1/2 to 2 hours, until apples are tender.

Spicy Black Bean Scrambled Eggs

Renae Scheiderer, Beallsville, OH

Festive Brunch Frittata

An easy, gourmet meal that will impress your guests...also try it with mushrooms and spinach.

Makes 6 servings

8 eggs
1/2 t. salt
1/8 t. pepper
1/2 c. shredded Cheddar cheese
2 T. butter
2 c. red, green and yellow
   peppers, chopped
1/4 c. onion, chopped

Beat together eggs, salt and pepper. Fold in cheese and set aside. Melt butter over medium heat in a 10" non-stick, oven-safe skillet. Add peppers and onion to skillet; sauté until tender. Pour eggs over peppers and onion; don't stir. Cover and cook over medium-low heat about 9 minutes. Eggs are set when frittata is lightly golden on the underside. Turn oven on broil. Move skillet from stovetop to oven; broil top about 5 inches from heat until lightly golden.

★ DOUBLE DUTY ★ Omelets and frittatas are perfect for using up all kinds of odds & ends from the fridge. Mushrooms, tomatoes and asparagus are especially good with eggs. Slice or dice veggies and sauté until tender...scrumptious!

Festive Brunch Frittata

Luna Crawley, London, OH

Garden-Fresh Frittata

Pick vegetables fresh from your garden for this delicious meal.

Makes 4 servings

3 egg whites
1 egg
2 T. fresh chives, chopped
1/8 t. salt
1/8 t. pepper
1/2 c. redskin potatoes, cubed
1/2 c. broccoli flowerets
1/4 c. yellow pepper, chopped
1/3 c. water
1/2 c. canola oil
Garnish: chopped fresh chives, diced tomatoes, shredded Cheddar cheese

Beat together egg whites, egg, chives, salt and pepper in a bowl until thoroughly combined; set aside. Add potatoes to a lightly greased ovenproof skillet over medium heat; sauté 5 to 6 minutes, until browned. Add broccoli, yellow pepper and water; cover skillet with lid. Cook 3 minutes, or until potatoes are tender; remove lid and allow liquid to evaporate. Add oil to skillet, thoroughly coating all vegetables. Pour egg mixture over vegetables; allow to set slightly, then stir. Cover skillet and cook frittata 3 minutes, or until eggs are set but not dry. Remove lid from skillet and place skillet under broiler, allowing top of frittata to brown. Garnish as desired.

★ SAVVY SECRET ★ To separate eggs when there's no egg separator handy, crack each egg into a cup and pour it through a slotted spoon. The egg white will run through the slots, leaving the yolk behind on the spoon.

Garden-Fresh Frittata

Regina Vining, Warwick, RI

Creamy Scrambled Eggs & Chives

Spoon onto buttered toast for scrambled egg sandwiches... a scrumptious light meal that's ready in a jiffy!

Makes 4 servings

8 eggs
2 T. fresh chives, chopped
1/2 t. salt
1/4 t. pepper
1/4 c. water
2 t. butter
1/2 c. cream cheese, diced

Whisk eggs together with chives, salt, pepper and water; set aside. Melt butter in a skillet over medium-high heat; pour in egg mixture. As eggs begin to set, push them gently toward center with a spatula so that uncooked egg can flow toward sides of skillet. When eggs are partially set, add cream cheese. Continue cooking for one more minute, or until eggs are set but still moist, stirring occasionally.

Carrie Kelderman, Pella, IA

Microwaved Scrambled Eggs

Got a hungry family? This is a quick recipe for making a large portion of scrambled eggs! It's terrific when you don't want to spend your time hovering over the stove.

Serves 6 to 8

1/4 c. butter, sliced
8 eggs, beaten
1/4 c. milk
1/4 c. grated Parmesan cheese
1/2 t. salt

Place butter in a large microwave-safe bowl. Microwave on high until butter melts. Meanwhile, in a separate bowl, whisk together remaining ingredients; add to butter and beat well. Microwave on high until eggs are set but slightly moist, 3 to 4 minutes. Remove from microwave. Cover and let stand until eggs are firm, 2 to 3 minutes. If eggs are still not set, return to microwave for 30 seconds.

Creamy Scrambled Eggs & Chives

Melissa Cassulis, Bridgewater, NY

Haystack Eggs

This is one of my dad's favorite breakfast treats. Mom has been making it for him for almost as long as I can remember!

Makes 4 servings

1-3/4 oz. can shoestring potatoes
4 eggs
1 c. shredded Cheddar cheese
6 slices bacon, crisply cooked and
    crumbled

Spread potatoes evenly over bottom of a greased 9" pie plate. Make 4 indentations in potatoes almost to bottom of pie plate. Carefully break one egg into each indentation. Bake at 350 degrees for 8 to 10 minutes, until eggs are almost set. Sprinkle with cheese and bacon. Return to oven; bake 2 to 4 more minutes, until eggs are set and cheese melts. Cut into 4 wedges; serve immediately.

Sandra Sullivan, Aurora, CO

Dilled Crab Egg Cups

A great dish for pop-up brunches and get-togethers.

Makes one dozen

1/2 lb. crabmeat, flaked
8-oz. pkg. cream cheese, diced
1 T. fresh dill, chopped and divided
1 doz. eggs
1/2 c. milk
1/2 c. sour cream
Optional: salad greens, favorite-
    flavor salad dressing

Divide crabmeat and cream cheese evenly among 12 greased muffin cups. Sprinkle dill into each cup. In a bowl, whisk together eggs, milk and sour cream. Divide egg mixture among muffin cups, filling each about 3/4 full. Bake at 450 degrees for 10 to 15 minutes, until puffed and golden. Cool slightly; remove from tin. Serve egg cups on a bed of salad greens drizzled with dressing, if desired.

Haystack Eggs

Connie Herek, Bay City, MI

Apple & Berry Breakfast Crisp

Use sliced strawberries instead of blueberries and it's just as tasty... and a dollop of vanilla yogurt on top makes it perfect!

Makes 9 servings

4 apples, peeled, cored and thinly sliced
2 c. blueberries
1/4 c. brown sugar, packed
1/4 c. frozen orange juice concentrate, thawed
2 T. all-purpose flour
1 t. cinnamon
Optional: vanilla yogurt

Combine all ingredients except yogurt in a large bowl; stir until fruit is evenly coated. Spoon into a lightly greased 8"x8" baking pan. Sprinkle Oat Topping evenly over fruit. Bake at 350 degrees for 30 to 35 minutes, until apples are tender. Serve warm with yogurt, if desired.

Oat Topping:

1 c. quick-cooking or long-cooking oats, uncooked
1/2 c. brown sugar, packed
1/3 c. butter, melted
2 T. all-purpose flour

Combine all ingredients; mix well.

★ HOT TIP ★ Warm caramel ice cream topping makes a delightful drizzle over crisps and cobblers. Just heat in the microwave for a few seconds, and it's ready.

Apple & Berry Breakfast Crisp

Stephanie Fackrell, Preston, ID

Apricot Oat Breakfast

Don't settle for ordinary oatmeal! Dried fruit, nuts and juice make these oats taste like dessert.

Serves 4 to 6

2 c. long-cooking oats, uncooked
1/3 c. slivered almonds
3/4 c. dried apricots, chopped
1/4 t. salt
1-1/2 c. orange juice
1 c. water
1/4 c. honey
Garnish: chopped apricots,
   slivered almonds
Optional: milk

Combine oats, nuts, dried apricots and salt together in a large bowl; set aside. Whisk together orange juice, water and honey; add to oat mixture. Refrigerate, covered, for 8 hours or overnight. Serve cold, garnished as desired.

Jackie Smulski, Lyons, IL

Scrambled Eggs & Lox

These eggs are sure to please everyone...they're excellent with toasted English muffins or bagels.

Makes 3 servings

6 eggs, beaten
1 T. fresh dill, minced
1 T. fresh chives, minced
1 T. green onion, minced
pepper to taste
2 T. butter
4-oz. pkg. smoked salmon, diced

Whisk together eggs, herbs, onion and pepper. Melt butter in a large skillet over medium heat. Add egg mixture and stir gently with a spatula until eggs begin to set. Stir in salmon; continue cooking until eggs reach desired doneness.

Apricot Oat Breakfast

Lily James, Fort Wayne, IN

Steak & Egg Hash

This is a hearty breakfast my family really loves.

Serves 3 to 6

1 to 2 T. olive oil
1-1/2 lbs. beef sirloin steak, cut
　into 1-inch cubes
1/4 t. salt
1/4 t. pepper
1/4 t. garlic powder
1 lb. potatoes, peeled and diced
1 onion, chopped
3 to 6 eggs
1 c. tomatoes, diced

Heat oil in a skillet over medium heat. Add beef cubes; sprinkle with seasonings. Cook beef cubes until no longer pink. Remove beef to a plate, reserving drippings in skillet. Add potatoes to skillet; cook until golden, stirring occasionally. Add onion; cook until soft and potatoes are cooked through. Return beef to skillet; reduce heat to low. With the back of a spoon, make 3 to 6 shallow wells in potato mixture; gently crack an egg into each well. Sprinkle with tomatoes. Cover and cook until eggs reach desired doneness.

★ TIME-SAVING SHORTCUT ★ When guests are coming for brunch, a little kitchen prep the night before is really helpful. Whisk up eggs for scrambling, dice meat and potatoes and lay out tableware ahead of time. In the morning, just tie on your prettiest apron and you'll be a relaxed hostess!

Steak & Egg Hash

Nadine Watson, Aurora, CO

Mexican Egg Bake

Refried beans make a perfect side for this dish.

Serves 8 to 10

12 corn tortillas, torn
16-oz. can green chili sauce
16-oz. pkg. shredded Cheddar
 cheese, divided
6 eggs
Garnish: sour cream, shredded
 lettuce and chopped tomato

Layer tortillas, chili sauce and 3/4 of cheese in an ungreased 13"x9" baking pan. Break eggs over top, spacing evenly. Sprinkle with remaining cheese. Bake, uncovered, at 350 degrees for 30 to 40 minutes. Slice into squares and garnish with sour cream, lettuce and tomato.

Carrie O'Shea, Marina del Rey, CA

Herbed Salmon Omelets

My husband's brother lives in Alaska, and last summer our family reunion was held there. The men went fishing all day, and the ladies crafted, shopped and tried to find new ways to prepare the bounty of fish being brought home! This recipe was one we enjoyed many times...it's delicious and couldn't be easier to make.

Makes 2 servings

1/4 c. sour cream
2 T. fresh dill, chopped
2 T. fresh chives, chopped
2 T. butter, divided
1/4 lb. smoked salmon, chopped
 and divided
6 eggs, beaten and divided

Mix together sour cream and herbs in a small bowl; set aside. Melt one tablespoon butter in a small skillet over low heat. Add half the salmon; cook and stir one minute. Add half the eggs to skillet and cook, lifting edges to allow uncooked egg to flow underneath. When almost set, spoon half the sour cream mixture over half the omelet. Fold other half over and slide onto plate. Keep warm while making second omelet with remaining ingredients.

Mexican Egg Bake

Summer Swiss Quiche, Page 108

CHAPTER THREE

Brunch-Bunch Favorites

Cream Cheese Enchiladas, Page 94

Classic Quiche Lorraine, Page 110

Margaret Sloan, Westerville, OH

Farm-Fresh Spinach Quiche

Add a sprinkle of nutmeg to the egg mixture if you like...it tastes wonderful with the spinach.

Makes 8 servings

8 slices bacon, crisply cooked, crumbled and divided
9-inch frozen pie crust, thawed
2 c. shredded Monterey Jack cheese
10-oz. pkg. frozen chopped spinach, thawed and drained
1-1/2 c. milk
3 eggs, beaten
1 T. all-purpose flour

Sprinkle half of crumbled bacon on bottom of pie crust. Mix together cheese, spinach, milk, eggs and flour. Pour over crust. Sprinkle remaining crumbled bacon on top. Bake at 350 degrees for one hour, or until center is set.

Vickie, Gooseberry Patch

Sausage Gravy & Biscuits

Enjoy these light and fluffy biscuits topped with hot sausage gravy any time of the day.

Serves 10 to 12

1/2 c. all-purpose flour
2 lbs. ground pork sausage, browned and drained
4 c. milk
salt and pepper to taste

In a medium saucepan over medium heat, sprinkle flour in with sausage, stirring until flour is dissolved. Gradually stir in milk and cook over medium heat until thick and bubbly. Season with salt and pepper; serve over warm Biscuits.

Biscuits:

4 c. self-rising flour
3 T. baking powder
2 T. sugar
7 T. shortening
2 c. buttermilk

Sift together flour, baking powder and sugar; cut in shortening. Mix in buttermilk with a fork, just until dough is moistened. Shape dough into a ball and knead a few times on a lightly floured surface. Roll out to 3/4-inch thickness and cut with a 3-inch biscuit cutter. Place biscuits on a greased baking sheet. Bake at 450 degrees for about 15 minutes or until golden. Makes 2 dozen.

Farm-Fresh Spinach Quiche

Athena Colegrove, Big Springs, TX

Impossibly Easy BLT Pie

I delighted my family one morning with this super-simple breakfast. We all like BLT's, so we really love this pie!

Makes 6 servings

12 slices bacon, crisply cooked and
   crumbled
1 c. shredded Swiss cheese
1/2 c. biscuit baking mix
1/3 c. plus 2 T. mayonnaise, divided
3/4 c. milk
1/8 t. pepper
2 eggs, beaten
1 c. shredded lettuce
6 thin slices tomato

Layer bacon and cheese in a lightly greased 9-inch pie plate. In a bowl, whisk together baking mix, 1/3 cup mayonnaise, milk, pepper and eggs until blended. Pour over cheese. Bake at 350 degrees for 25 to 30 minutes, until top is golden and a knife inserted in center comes out clean. Let stand 5 minutes. Spread remaining mayonnaise over pie. Sprinkle with lettuce; arrange tomato slices over lettuce.

Traci Green, Orange Park, FL

Hashbrown Breakfast Pizza

Let the kids help put together this fun breakfast dish...they'll love eating their creation.

Makes 6 servings

8-oz. tube refrigerated crescent rolls
1 lb. ground pork sausage, browned
   and drained
1 c. shredded Cheddar cheese
2 T. grated Parmesan cheese
1 c. frozen shredded hashbrowns,
   thawed
5 eggs, beaten
1/4 c. milk
1/2 t. salt
1/8 t. pepper

Separate rolls and press together to form a crust on an ungreased 12" pizza pan. Layer with sausage, cheeses and hashbrowns; set aside. Whisk eggs, milk, salt and pepper together and pour over hashbrowns. Bake at 375 degrees for 30 minutes. Cut into wedges.

Impossibly Easy BLT Pie

Sharon Demers, Dolores, CO

Sausage & Cherry Tart with Walnuts

The tart fruit pairs beautifully with the spicy sausage. Your guests will love this!

Makes 8 servings

1 c. all-purpose flour
2/3 c. walnuts, ground
6 T. chilled butter, cubed
1 T. sugar
1/2 t. dry mustard
1/4 t. salt
1/8 t. cayenne pepper
1 to 2 T. milk
1/2 lb. ground pork breakfast sausage
1 onion, finely diced
1/2 to 1 c. dried tart cherries or cranberries
1/2 c. chopped walnuts
1/4 t. dried thyme
2 eggs, beaten
1 c. whipping cream
3-oz. pkg. crumbled Gorgonzola cheese

Combine flour, ground walnuts, butter, sugar, dry mustard, salt and cayenne pepper in a food processor. Pulse just until mixture resembles bread crumbs. Add one tablespoon milk; pulse until dough comes together. If dough is too crumbly, add more milk until it holds together. Shape dough into a ball and press evenly into a lightly greased 9" round tart pan. Freeze for 30 minutes. Bake crust at 350 degrees for 15 to 20 minutes, until golden. Remove from oven and set aside. Brown sausage and onion in a skillet over medium heat; drain well. Stir in cherries or cranberries, walnuts and thyme. Set aside. Whisk eggs and cream in a bowl until smooth. Spoon sausage mixture into baked crust; sprinkle with cheese. Pour egg mixture over all. Bake at 350 degrees for 15 to 20 minutes, until golden and a toothpick inserted in center comes out clean. Cool 15 minutes before serving.

★ SAVVY SIDE ★ Mini tarts are perfect for a brunch buffet. Simply press dough gently into ungreased muffin cups, and follow the rest of the recipe. Baking times will be shorter, so check tarts after 10 minutes.

Sausage & Cherry Tart with Walnuts

Vickie, Gooseberry Patch

Tex-Mex Sausage Casserole

A slow-cooker casserole that's ideal for a breakfast with family & friends. For a real kick, add chopped jalapeños to taste!

Makes 10 servings

1-lb. pkg. ground breakfast sausage, browned and drained
4-oz. can diced green chiles
1 onion, diced
1 green pepper, diced
2-1/2 c. shredded Monterey Jack or Pepper Jack cheese
18 eggs, beaten
Garnish: sour cream, salsa, chopped fresh cilantro, chopped green onions

Layer half each of sausage, chiles, onion, pepper and cheese in a greased 6-quart slow cooker. Repeat layering. Pour beaten eggs over top. Cover and cook on low setting for 7 to 8 hours. Serve with sour cream and salsa, and garnish with cilantro and green onions.

Patty Schroyer, Baxter, IA

Zesty Brunch Quiche

Try using peach or apricot salsa for a whole new taste.

Makes 6 servings

1 c. shredded Cheddar cheese
4 slices bacon, crisply cooked and crumbled
2 green onions, thinly sliced
9-inch frozen pie crust
3 eggs, beaten
1/2 c. milk
1/2 c. salsa

Sprinkle cheese, bacon and onions into pie crust; set aside. Whisk eggs, milk and salsa together; pour into pie crust. Carefully place on a baking sheet; bake at 375 degrees for 35 minutes. Let stand 10 minutes before slicing.

Tex-Mex Sausage Casserole

Jena Buckler, Bloomington Springs, TN

Company Breakfast Casserole

For Southwestern flair, replace the mushrooms with a small can of sliced olives, add Monterey Jack cheese instead of Cheddar and serve with spicy salsa on the side.

Serves 8 to 10

16-oz. pkg. frozen shredded
  hashbrowns, thawed and divided
1 onion, chopped and divided
1 lb. ground pork sausage, browned
  and drained
1 green pepper, chopped
4-oz. can sliced mushrooms, drained
1/2 to 1 c. shredded Cheddar cheese,
  divided
1 doz. eggs, beaten
1-1/2 c. milk
salt and pepper to taste
Optional: garlic salt to taste

Spread half the hashbrowns in a lightly greased 13"x9" baking pan. Layer ingredients as follows: half the onion, sausage, remaining onion, green pepper, mushrooms and half the cheese. In a separate bowl, whisk together eggs, milk and seasonings. Pour egg mixture over casserole; top with remaining hashbrowns and remaining cheese. Cover with aluminum foil and refrigerate overnight. Bake, covered, at 350 degrees for 45 to 60 minutes. Uncover and bake an additional 20 minutes, or until a knife inserted in center comes out clean.

★ TIME-SAVING SHORTCUT ★ On busy weekends when you've got overnight company, a simple make-ahead casserole is perfect. Assemble it the night before and refrigerate, then pop it in the oven the next morning. You'll have plenty of time to chat with your guests!

Company Breakfast Casserole

Dale Duncan, Waterloo, IA

Bacon & Egg Potato Skins

A tummy-filling complete meal in a potato skin...yummy!

Makes 4 servings

2 baking potatoes
4 eggs, beaten
1 to 2 t. butter
salt and pepper to taste
1/4 c. shredded Monterey Jack cheese
1/4 c. shredded Cheddar cheese
4 slices bacon, crisply cooked and crumbled
Garnish: sour cream, chopped fresh chives

Bake potatoes at 400 degrees for one hour, until tender. Slice potatoes in half lengthwise; scoop out centers and reserve for another recipe. Place potato skins on a lightly greased baking sheet. Bake at 400 degrees for 6 to 8 minutes, until crisp. In a skillet over medium heat, scramble eggs in butter just until they begin to set. Add salt and pepper; remove from heat. Spoon equal amounts of eggs, cheeses and bacon into each potato skin. Reduce heat to 350 degrees and bake for 7 to 10 minutes, until cheese is melted and eggs are completely set. Garnish with sour cream and chives.

★ SAVVY SIDE ★ **These potato skins are so easy to customize for a family get-together. Set out little bowls of salsa, sautéed peppers, onions and mushrooms. Let your guests add their own toppings!**

Bacon & Egg Potato Skins

Jackie Balla, Walbridge, OH

Country-Style Breakfast Pizza

A surefire breakfast hit...you'll get requests for this recipe!

Makes 8 servings

13.8-oz. tube refrigerated pizza crust dough
Optional: garlic salt to taste
24-oz. pkg. refrigerated mashed potatoes
10 eggs, beaten
Optional: chopped vegetables, cooked ham or sausage
8-oz. pkg. shredded Colby Jack cheese
4-oz. pkg. crumbled bacon pieces
Garnish: sliced tomatoes, diced green onion

Spread pizza dough in a pizza pan sprayed with non-stick vegetable spray; sprinkle with garlic salt, if desired, and set aside. Place mashed potatoes in a microwave-safe bowl; microwave on high setting for about 3 minutes, until heated through. Spread potatoes over dough. Cook eggs as desired, adding vegetables, ham or sausage, if desired. Spread egg mixture evenly over potatoes. Sprinkle with cheese; top with bacon. Bake at 350 degrees for 22 to 25 minutes, until cheese is melted and crust is golden. Garnish with sliced tomatoes and green onions.

★ HOT TIP ★ Add some extra flavor to those refrigerated mashed potatoes! Heat up potatoes, blend in sour cream and cream cheese to taste, then heat up again until well blended. Delicious in Country-Style Breakfast Pizza!

Country-Style Breakfast Pizza

Joyce Boswell, Lewisport, KY

Southern-Style Breakfast Casserole

If I didn't bring this to breakfast on Palm Sunday, I don't think they'd let me in the door!

Serves 8 to 10

2 lbs. ground pork breakfast sausage, browned and drained
4 eggs, beaten
1 onion, diced
6 c. crispy rice cereal
2 c. cooked rice
10-3/4 oz. can cream of chicken soup
10-3/4 oz. can cream of celery soup
8-oz. pkg. shredded Cheddar cheese
1/2 c. milk

Combine all ingredients in a large bowl. Pour into a lightly greased 13"x9" baking pan. Bake, uncovered, at 400 degrees for 30 minutes.

Gail Blain, Hastings, NE

Ham Steak & Apples Skillet

My grandmother's old black cast-iron skillet brings back wonderful memories of the delicious things she used to make in it. I seek out scrumptious skillet recipes just so I can use Grandma's old skillet... this one has become a real favorite at our house!

Makes 6 servings

3 T. butter
1/2 c. brown sugar, packed
1 T. Dijon mustard
2 c. apples, cored and sliced
2 1-lb. bone-in ham steaks

Melt butter in a large skillet over medium heat. Add brown sugar and mustard; bring to a simmer. Add apples; cover and simmer 5 minutes. Top apples with ham steaks. Cover and simmer 10 more minutes, or until apples are tender. Remove ham to a platter and cut into serving-size pieces. Top ham with apples and sauce.

Southern-Style Breakfast Casserole

Georgia Cooper, Helena, MT

Ham-and-Tomato Pie

Summer's best flavors are blended in this quiche-style recipe...sweet fresh basil, juicy plum tomatoes and crisp green onions.

Makes 6 servings

8-oz. pkg. cooked ham, diced
1/2 c. green onions, sliced
9-inch frozen pie crust, thawed
1 T. Dijon mustard
1 c. shredded mozzarella cheese, divided
2 plum tomatoes, thinly sliced
1 egg
1/3 c. half-and-half
1 T. fresh basil, chopped
1/8 t. pepper

Sauté ham and green onions in a large non-stick skillet over medium heat 5 minutes, or until ham is browned and any liquid evaporates. Brush bottom of pie crust evenly with mustard; sprinkle with 1/2 cup mozzarella cheese. Spoon ham mixture evenly over cheese and top with sliced tomatoes arranged in a single layer. Beat egg and half-and-half with a fork until blended; pour over tomatoes. Sprinkle evenly with basil, pepper and remaining 1/2 cup cheese. Bake on lowest oven rack at 425 degrees for 20 to 23 minutes, until lightly golden and set. Cool on a wire rack 20 minutes. Cut into wedges to serve.

★ TIME-SAVING SHORTCUT ★ **Toss a few refrigerated pie crusts in the cart the next time you're grocery shopping...they're such time savers in either savory or sweet pie recipes!**

Ham-and-Tomato Pie

Mary Kathryn Carter, Platte City, MO

Cream Cheese Enchiladas

This creamy variation on Mexican enchiladas is yummy! It won me 1st place in a local newspaper's holiday cooking contest. For a brunch twist, use breakfast sausage instead of ground beef.

Makes 8 servings

2 8-oz. pkgs. cream cheese, softened
1 c. sour cream
2 10-oz. cans mild green chile
   enchilada sauce
1/4 c. jalapeños, chopped
1 lb. ground beef, browned and
   drained
1/2 c. shredded sharp Cheddar cheese
8 to 12 flour tortillas
1 sweet onion, chopped
1/2 c. sliced black olives
Garnish: sliced black olives, chopped
   tomato, shredded lettuce, chopped
   green onion

Blend together cream cheese, sour cream, enchilada sauce and jalapeños in a large bowl; set aside. Combine ground beef and shredded cheese in another bowl; set aside. Fill each tortilla with one to 2 tablespoons cream cheese mixture and one to 2 tablespoons beef mixture. Sprinkle each with onion and olives; roll up tortillas. Place in a 13"x9" baking pan; cover with remaining cream cheese mixture. Bake, uncovered, at 400 degrees for 30 to 40 minutes; cover if top begins to brown. Garnish with olives, tomatoes, lettuce and green onions.

★ SAVVY SIDE ★ **Looking for an easy breakfast side? For breakfast in a dash, pick up packages of heat & serve hashbrowns... real time-savers on busy days.**

Cream Cheese Enchiladas

Janine Kuras, Warren, MI

Cheesy Spinach Pie

Two cheeses combine to make this dish delectable.

Makes 8 servings

2 c. cottage cheese
2/3 c. crumbled feta cheese
1/4 t. pepper
10-oz. pkg. frozen chopped spinach, thawed and drained
3 eggs, beaten
1/4 c. butter, melted
2 T. all-purpose flour
2 t. dried, minced onion

In a large bowl, combine ingredients in order listed; mix well. Spread in a greased 1-1/2 quart casserole dish. Bake, uncovered, at 350 degrees for 45 minutes, or until center is set.

Jessica Robertson, Fishers, IN

Slow-Cooker Hashbrown Casserole

Sometimes I'll substitute bacon or ham in place of the sausage. This hearty recipe works best in a large, oval slow-cooker.

Makes 8 servings

32-oz. pkg. frozen shredded hashbrowns
1 lb. ground pork sausage, browned and drained
1 onion, diced
1 green pepper, diced
1-1/2 c. shredded Cheddar cheese
1 doz. eggs, beaten
1 c. milk
1 t. salt
1 t. pepper

Place 1/3 each of hashbrowns, sausage, onion, green pepper and cheese in a lightly greased slow cooker. Repeat layering 2 more times, ending with cheese. Beat eggs, milk, salt and pepper together in a large bowl; pour over top. Cover and cook on low setting for 8 to 10 hours, until set.

Cheesy Spinach Pie

Vivian Baker, Centerville, OH

Cheesy Ham Strata

Put together the night before, this makes a great dish for celebrations and brunch!

Makes 8 servings

12 slices bread, crusts trimmed
3/4 lb. Cheddar cheese, sliced
10-oz. pkg. frozen chopped broccoli,
   cooked
2 c. cooked ham, cubed
2 T. dried, minced onion
6 eggs, beaten
3-1/2 c. milk
1/2 t. salt
1/4 t. dry mustard
1/2 c. shredded Cheddar cheese

Cut out desired shapes from center of each bread slice using cookie cutters; set aside the cut-out shapes and place the remaining bread in a greased 13"x9" baking pan. Layer Cheddar cheese slices over bread pieces; spread broccoli and ham over cheese slices. Sprinkle with onion; arrange cut-out shapes on top. Combine eggs, milk, salt and mustard in a bowl and blend well; pour over top of strata. Cover and refrigerate overnight. Bake, uncovered, at 325 degrees for one hour 5 minutes, or until set, sprinkling with shredded Cheddar cheese the last 5 minutes of baking. Let stand 10 minutes before serving.

★ HOT TIP ★ If weekdays are busy, why not enjoy a brunch-for-two on the weekend? Relax with each other over tea & coffee, a basket of muffins and a savory baked strata. You'll be glad you did!

Cheesy Ham Strata

April Jacobs, Loveland, CO

Turkey-Veggie Bagels

Instead of bagels, you can also slice a loaf of round bread in half and layer on all the goodies. Replace the top of the loaf, cut into wedges and secure the sandwich in plastic wrap...an easy take-along breakfast.

Makes 4 servings

4 onion bagels, sliced in half
4 leaves romaine lettuce
8 slices deli smoked turkey
1 cucumber, thinly sliced
2 to 4 radishes, thinly sliced
1 to 2 carrots, peeled and shredded
1/4 c. cream cheese with chives and
    onions

Arrange 4 bagel halves on a serving tray. Place a lettuce leaf on each; top with turkey, cucumber, radish and carrot. Spread cream cheese on top halves of bagels; place on bottom halves.

Janine Kuras, Warren, MI

Crustless Bacon-Swiss Quiche

With one less step, this quiche recipe is a real time-saver.

Makes 12 servings

9 eggs, beaten
3 c. milk
1 t. dry mustard
salt and pepper to taste
9 slices white bread, crusts
    trimmed
1-1/2 c. Swiss cheese, diced
1 lb. bacon, crisply cooked and
    crumbled

Combine eggs, milk, mustard, salt and pepper in a large bowl; blend well. Tear bread into small pieces; add to egg mixture along with cheese and bacon. Spoon into a greased 13"x9" baking pan or 2 greased 9" glass pie plates. Cover and refrigerate 2 hours to overnight. Uncover and bake at 350 degrees for 45 to 50 minutes, until eggs have set. Cut into squares or wedges.

Turkey-Veggie Bagels

Holly Stockwell, Gahanna, OH

Holly's Broccoli, Ham & Cheese Strata

A perfect holiday brunch for those you love.

Serves 8 to 10

14 slices white or wheat bread, crusts trimmed
1-1/2 c. shredded Cheddar cheese
10-oz. pkg. frozen chopped broccoli, thawed and drained
1/4 c. onion, chopped
1 c. cooked ham, chopped
1 tomato, chopped
5 eggs
1 t. seasoned salt
1/2 t. garlic powder
1/2 t. mustard
1/2 t. cayenne pepper
1-1/2 c. milk

Butter a 13"×9" baking pan. Layer 7 slices of bread on bottom of pan. Sprinkle half of cheese over bread slices. Next, layer thawed chopped broccoli, onion, ham and tomato over cheese. Top with remaining cheese and bread slices. In a mixing bowl, combine remaining ingredients; beat well. Pour egg mixture over layered ingredients in baking pan. Cover and refrigerate at least 3 hours or overnight. Bake, uncovered, at 350 degrees for 40 to 50 minutes, until a toothpick inserted in center comes out clean.

★ SAVVY SECRET ★ Apples speed ripening of tomatoes, peaches, pears and avocados when stored together in a brown bag. Set in a warm dark place and punch a few holes in the bag for ventilation.

Holly's Broccoli, Ham & Cheese Strata

Janice O'Brien, Warrenton, VA

Summery Herbed Tomato Pie

A refrigerated pie crust makes this one quick-to-fix dish.

Serves 8 to 10

9-inch pie crust
3 to 4 tomatoes, sliced
1/2 c. fresh chives, chopped
2 T. fresh basil, chopped
salt and pepper to taste
2 c. shredded mozzarella cheese
1/2 c. mayonnaise
Garnish: additional fresh chives and
  basil, chopped

Press pie crust into a 9" pie plate. Bake at 425 degrees for 5 minutes. Reduce oven to 400 degrees. Arrange tomato slices in crust; sprinkle with chives, basil, salt and pepper. Combine cheese and mayonnaise; spread over tomatoes. Bake at 400 degrees for 35 minutes. Garnish with additional chives and basil.

Jill Ball, Highland, UT

Breakfast Bruschetta

My family loves bruschetta, so I thought, why not have it for breakfast?

Makes 4 servings

1 c. red or green grapes, sliced
1 c. strawberries, hulled and sliced
1/4 t. cinnamon
1/8 t. nutmeg
1 c. cottage cheese or ricotta
1 T. chopped walnuts
1 baguette, cut in half lengthwise and
  sliced into 1-inch diagonals
2 to 3 T. olive oil

Place fruit in a small bowl; sprinkle with cinnamon and nutmeg. In another bowl, mix cheese and nuts. Brush bread lightly with olive oil and place on an ungreased baking sheet. Bake at 450 degrees until the bread turns golden, about 3 minutes. Remove from oven and spread cheese mixture on each piece of bread. Top with fruit mixture.

Summery Herbed Tomato Pie

Donna Deeds, Marysville, TN

Chicken-Fried Steak

Authentic chicken-fried steak is crunchy outside, tender inside and served with plenty of cream gravy!

Makes 6 servings

2-1/4 t. salt, divided
1-3/4 t. pepper, divided
6 4-oz. beef cube steaks
1 sleeve saltine crackers, crushed
1-1/4 c. all-purpose flour, divided
1/2 t. baking powder
1/2 t. cayenne pepper
4-3/4 c. milk, divided
2 eggs
3-1/2 c. peanut oil

Sprinkle 1/4 teaspoon each salt and pepper over steaks. Set aside. Combine cracker crumbs, one cup flour, baking powder, one teaspoon salt, 1/2 teaspoon pepper and cayenne pepper. Whisk together 3/4 cup milk and eggs. Dredge steaks in cracker crumb mixture; dip in milk mixture and dredge in cracker mixture again. Pour oil into a 12-inch skillet; heat to 360 degrees. (Do not use a non-stick skillet.) Fry steaks, in batches, 10 minutes. Turn and fry each batch 4 to 5 more minutes, until golden brown. Remove to a wire rack on a jelly-roll pan. Keep steaks warm in a 225-degree oven. Carefully drain hot oil, reserving cooked bits and one tablespoon drippings in skillet. Whisk together remaining 1/4 cup flour, one teaspoon salt, one teaspoon pepper and 4 cups milk. Pour mixture into reserved drippings in skillet; cook over medium-high heat, whisking constantly, 10 to 12 minutes, until thickened. Serve gravy with steak.

★ TIME-SAVING SHORTCUT ★ What to serve with your Chicken-Fried Steak? Cook up a crock of overnight grits...creamy and perfect every time! Following the package directions, add the desired amount of long-cooking grits to a slow cooker and twice the amount of water as specified. Sprinkle with salt. Cover and cook on low setting for 7 to 8 hours, stirring in more water toward the end of cooking time, if needed. Top with butter, shredded cheese or a splash of cream.

Chicken-Fried Steak

Rebecca Barna, Blairsville, PA

Summer Swiss Quiche

This is an excellent breakfast or brunch dish to serve when the garden harvest kicks in.

Serves 8 to 10

1/2 lb. bacon
2 zucchini, thinly sliced
1 green pepper, chopped
1 onion, chopped
8 eggs, beaten
1 c. milk
1/4 c. biscuit baking mix
6 slices Swiss cheese

Cook bacon in a skillet over medium heat until crisp; remove from pan and set aside. Sauté zucchini, green pepper and onion in bacon drippings in same skillet over medium heat. Mix eggs, milk and baking mix in a bowl. Pour egg mixture into a lightly greased 13"x9" baking pan. Spoon zucchini mixture over egg mixture. Cover with crumbled bacon; arrange cheese slices on top. Bake, uncovered, at 350 degrees for 30 to 35 minutes, until a toothpick inserted in center comes out clean. Cut into squares.

Ursula Juarez-Wall, Dumfries, VA

Sausage & Jack Pie

Here's a quick and tasty breakfast dish that will satisfy any hungry family... my four girls make short work of it!

Serves 8 to 10

2 8-oz. tubes refrigerated crescent rolls
2 8-oz. pkgs. brown & serve breakfast sausage links, browned and sliced
4 c. shredded Monterey Jack or Colby Jack cheese
8 eggs, beaten
1-1/2 c. milk
2 T. onion, chopped
2 T. green pepper, chopped
1/2 t. salt
1/4 t. pepper
1/4 t. dried oregano

Separate each can of crescent rolls into 2 large rectangles. Place rectangles side-by-side in an ungreased 13"x9" baking pan to form a crust, covering bottom and halfway up sides of pan. Press to seal perforations. Arrange sausages over crust; sprinkle with cheese. Combine remaining ingredients and pour over cheese. Bake, uncovered, at 400 degrees for 20 to 25 minutes.

Summer Swiss Quiche

Francie Stutzman, Clinton, OH

Classic Quiche Lorraine

This recipe makes two quiches... just add a fresh fruit salad for an oh-so-easy brunch with friends.

Makes 2 quiches; each serves 6

1 lb. bacon, cut into 1-inch pieces
2 9-inch pie crusts
8-oz. pkg. shredded Swiss cheese
8-oz. pkg. shredded Cheddar cheese
8 eggs, beaten
2 c. whipping cream
1 T. Worcestershire sauce
1 T. pepper
1/8 t. salt

Cook bacon in a skillet over medium-high heat until crisp; drain on paper towels. Arrange pie crusts in two 9-inch pie plates; sprinkle bacon into crusts. Mix together cheeses in a bowl; sprinkle over bacon. Whisk together remaining ingredients in a separate bowl. Divide egg mixture between crusts. Bake at 350 degrees for 45 minutes, or until golden. Let stand about 10 minutes; cut into wedges and serve warm.

Jo Ann, Gooseberry Patch

Garlic Mushrooms on Toast

An elegant light breakfast dish...good made with plain button mushrooms or a mixture of portabella and cremini mushrooms. If you have a secret place to hunt morel mushrooms, they would be yummy in this recipe.

Serves 4 to 6

2 slices bacon, chopped
1-1/2 lbs. mushrooms, stemmed and sliced
2 cloves garlic, minced
1/2 t. dried rosemary
1/4 t. salt
pepper to taste
Optional: 1/4 c. white wine
4 to 6 slices bread, toasted, buttered and halved diagonally

In a skillet over medium heat, cook bacon until partially done but not crisp. Add mushrooms, garlic and seasonings. Cook, stirring occasionally, for 8 to 10 minutes, until most of the liquid has evaporated. Pour in wine, if using; cook and stir for an additional minute. Spoon mushroom mixture over toast triangles.

Classic Quiche Lorraine

Bruce Benton, Tampa, FL

Fried Egg & Cheese Burger

When it's my turn to cook breakfast, this is what I like to make. The kids love having cheeseburgers for breakfast!

Makes 8 servings

1 lb. bacon
2 lbs. ground beef
1/2 t. salt
1/4 t. pepper
1/4 t. garlic powder
8 hamburger buns
8 eggs
Optional: 1 T. butter
8 hamburger buns, split
8 slices cheese
Garnish: lettuce leaves, sliced onion,
   sliced tomato, pickle chips

In a large skillet over medium heat, cook bacon until crisp; drain and set aside. Meanwhile, in a large bowl, sprinkle beef with seasonings; form into 8 patties. In the same skillet over medium heat, cook patties until no longer pink inside. Drain and set aside. Gently crack 4 eggs into the same skillet, adding butter if desired. Cook over medium-low heat until whites are set and yolks are partially cooked; set aside. Cook remaining eggs. To serve, top the bottom of each bun with a beef patty and a cheese slice; place on a broiler pan. Broil until cheese is melted. Top each with one fried egg and 2 slices bacon; add desired garnishes and top halves of buns.

★ HOT TIP ★ Burger buns just taste better toasted...and they won't get soggy! Butter buns lightly and place them on a hot grill for 30 seconds to one minute on each side, until toasty.

Fried Egg & Cheese Burger

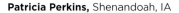

Beth Kramer, Port Saint Lucie, FL

Flatbread Breakfast Pizza

My teenagers love to whip up these little breakfast pizzas. Sometimes we'll add leftover crispy bacon too...yum!

Makes one serving

1 egg, beaten
1 T. milk
1 brown & serve breakfast sausage link or patty, browned and chopped
6-inch round flatbread
2 T. finely shredded Cheddar cheese

In a greased 2-cup microwave-safe bowl, whisk together egg and milk; stir in sausage. Microwave on high for 30 seconds; use a spoon to push cooked edges toward center. Microwave for 15 to 45 seconds, until egg is almost set. Turn out egg and slice into 4 to 5 pieces; arrange on flatbread. Sprinkle with cheese. Microwave an additional 10 to 15 seconds, until cheese melts.

Patricia Perkins, Shenandoah, IA

Ham & Shrimp Risotto

Add a little more hot pepper sauce if you like it extra spicy!

Serves 4 to 6

2 T. butter
7-oz. pkg. chicken-flavored rice vermicelli mix, uncooked
2-3/4 c. water
2 c. cooked ham, diced
1 lb. cooked, peeled medium shrimp
1/4 c. celery, diced
1/4 c. green pepper, diced
1 T. dried, minced onion
1/4 t. hot pepper sauce
1/4 t. pepper

Melt butter in a large saucepan over medium heat. Add uncooked rice vermicelli mix and sauté just until golden. Stir in remaining ingredients; reduce heat, cover and simmer for 15 minutes.

Flatbread Breakfast Pizza

Gingerbread Waffles, Page 124

CHAPTER FOUR

Pancakes, French Toast & Waffles

Blueberry-Lemon Crepes, Page 132

Florence's Buttermilk Pancakes, Page 140

Lela Wingerson, Omaha, NE

Good Morning Pumpkin Pancakes

Don't wait 'til autumn to enjoy this delicious breakfast treat!

Makes 12 to 16 pancakes

2 c. biscuit baking mix
2 T. brown sugar, packed
2 t. cinnamon
1 t. allspice
12-oz. can evaporated milk
1/2 c. canned pumpkin
2 eggs, beaten
2 t. oil
1 t. vanilla extract

Combine biscuit mix, brown sugar and spices in a large bowl. Add remaining ingredients; beat until smooth. Pour 1/4 to 1/2 cup batter for each pancake onto a greased hot griddle; cook until top surface is bubbly and edges are dry. Turn over; cook until golden. Serve with Pumpkin-Maple Syrup.

Pumpkin-Maple Syrup:

1 c. maple syrup
1-1/4 c. canned pumpkin
1/4 t. cinnamon

Combine all ingredients together in a small saucepan. Mix well and warm through over low heat. Makes about 2 cups.

Lori Ritchey, Denver, PA

Southern Cornmeal Waffles

I live in the northeast and occasionally we get a hankering for something southern. This waffle recipe is easy and delicious... perfect with country ham.

Makes 4 to 6 waffles

3/4 c. yellow cornmeal
2 T. all-purpose flour
1 t. sugar
1/2 t. baking powder
1/4 t. baking soda
1/4 t. salt
1 egg, beaten
1 c. milk
1/4 c. oil
2 t. lemon juice

In a bowl, mix together cornmeal, flour, sugar, baking powder, baking soda and salt. Stir in remaining ingredients. Drop batter by 1/2 cupfuls onto a lightly greased hot waffle iron. Bake according to manufacturer's directions.

Good Morning Pumpkin Pancakes

Vickie, Gooseberry Patch

Dutch Puffed Apple Pancake

An old-fashioned favorite that puffs up high in the oven and then falls when taken out...fun to make, delicious to eat!

Makes 4 servings

1/4 c. butter, melted
1 Granny Smith apple, peeled, cored
   and thinly sliced
1/2 c. chopped walnuts
4 eggs
1 c. milk
2/3 c. all-purpose flour
2 T. sugar
1 t. vanilla extract
1/4 t. cinnamon
1/8 t. salt
1/2 c. sweetened, dried cranberries
3 T. brown sugar, packed
Optional: maple syrup

Spread butter in a 9" glass pie plate; arrange apple slices and walnuts over butter. Bake at 425 degrees for about 5 minutes, until apples begin to soften and walnuts are lightly toasted. Beat together eggs, milk, flour, sugar, vanilla, cinnamon and salt in a large bowl with an electric mixer at medium speed. Stir in cranberries. Remove pie plate from oven; spray inside edges with non-stick vegetable spray. Pour batter over apples and walnuts; sprinkle with brown sugar. Bake, uncovered, at 425 degrees for about 25 minutes, until center is set and edges are puffed and golden. Cut into wedges and serve immediately with maple syrup, if desired.

Heather Nagel, Cleveland, OH

Apple-Sausage Pancakes

I first had these at my friend Beth's house for brunch. They were so good! A couple years later at my bridal shower, I was so happy to find this recipe taped to the griddle she bought me as a gift.

Makes one dozen pancakes

1/2 lb. ground pork breakfast
   sausage
1 egg, beaten
1 c. pancake mix
2/3 c. oil
1/2 t. cinnamon
1/2 c. apple, cored and shredded

Brown sausage in a skillet over medium heat; drain. Meanwhile, in a bowl, mix together egg, pancake mix, oil and cinnamon. Fold in sausage and apple. Drop batter by 1/2 cupfuls onto a hot greased griddle. Cook until golden on both sides. Serve with Apple Syrup.

Apple Syrup:

1 c. apple cider or apple juice
1/2 c. sugar
3 T. butter, sliced
1 T. cornstarch
1 T. lemon juice
1/8 t. pumpkin pie spice

Combine all ingredients in a saucepan over medium-high heat. Stir well and bring to a boil. Reduce heat to low; keep warm until ready to serve.

Dutch Puffed Apple Pancake

Gloria Bills, Plymouth, MI

Overnight Blueberry French Toast

This delicious recipe has become a holiday tradition at our house...my husband and children love it! It's easy to make the night before; then in the morning, just pop it in the oven.

Serves 6 to 8

1 baguette loaf, sliced 1-inch thick
6 eggs
3 c. milk
1 c. brown sugar, packed and divided
vanilla extract to taste
nutmeg to taste
1/4 c. chopped pecans
2 c. blueberries
Optional: maple syrup

Arrange baguette slices in a lightly greased 13"x9" baking pan; set aside. Whisk together eggs, milk, 3/4 cup brown sugar, vanilla and nutmeg in a large bowl. Pour mixture evenly over baguette slices. Cover and chill overnight. Just before baking, sprinkle remaining brown sugar, pecans and blueberries over top. Bake, uncovered, at 350 degrees for 50 minutes, or until golden and bubbly. Serve with maple syrup, as desired.

Gladys Kielar, Whitehouse, OH

Birthday Baked French Swirl Toast

We've enjoyed this baked French toast for birthday breakfasts. It's a great choice for any special day and when guests come for an overnight visit.

Makes 8 servings

16-oz. loaf cinnamon swirl bread, cubed
3/4 c. sweetened dried cranberries
6 eggs, beaten
3 c. half-and-half or milk
2 t. vanilla extract
Garnish: cinnamon-sugar or powdered sugar, whipped butter, maple syrup

Combine bread cubes and cranberries in a greased shallow 3-quart casserole dish. In a bowl, whisk together eggs, half-and-half or milk and vanilla; pour over bread mixture. Cover and refrigerate for one hour to overnight. Uncover; bake at 350 degrees for 45 minutes, or until golden and set in the center. Sprinkle with cinnamon-sugar or powdered sugar. Serve topped with whipped butter and maple syrup.

Overnight Blueberry French Toast

Robin Hill, Rochester, NY

Gingerbread Waffles

Breakfast just doesn't get any
better than this!

Makes one dozen waffles

2 c. all-purpose flour
1 t. baking soda
1 t. baking powder
1 t. ground ginger
1/2 t. cinnamon
1/4 t. ground cloves
2 t. fresh ginger, peeled and minced
1/4 t. salt
1/4 t. pepper
2 eggs
1/4 c. sugar
1 c. milk
1/2 c. molasses
6 T. butter, melted
2 T. oil
1 T. lemon juice
Garnish: whipped cream, warmed
   syrup

Combine first 9 ingredients in a
large bowl; mix well and set aside.
In a small bowl, whisk together
remaining ingredients except
garnish. Add egg mixture gradually
to flour mixture; stir until well
blended. Bake until golden in a lightly
greased waffle iron, according to
manufacturer's instructions. Serve
warm with whipped cream or syrup,
as desired.

Jennifer Bontrager, Oklahoma City, OK

Yummy Blueberry Waffles

When I was a little girl, my grandpa
owned a blueberry farm. The berries
were so delicious that we always
took home several gallons when our
summer visit was over. This waffle
recipe cooks up nice and fluffy...and
the farm-fresh blueberries only make
them better!

Makes 4 waffles

2 eggs
2 c. all-purpose flour
1-3/4 c. milk
1/2 c. oil
1 T. sugar
4 t. baking powder
1/4 t. salt
1/2 t. vanilla extract
1 to 1-1/2 c. blueberries

In a large bowl, beat eggs with
an electric mixer on medium
speed until fluffy. Add remaining
ingredients except berries; beat
just until smooth. Spray a waffle
iron with non-stick vegetable spray.
Pour batter by 1/2 cupfuls onto the
preheated waffle iron. Scatter desired
amount of berries over batter. Bake
according to manufacturer's
directions, until golden.

Gingerbread Waffles

Alice Collins, Kansas City, MO

Overnight Apple French Toast

Serve with bacon or sausage on the side, or fresh orange slices and strawberries.

Serves 6 to 8

1 c. brown sugar, packed
1/2 c. butter
2 T. light corn syrup
4 Granny Smith apples, peeled, cored and sliced 1/4-inch thick
3 eggs
1 c. milk
1 t. vanilla extract
9 slices day-old French bread

In a small saucepan, combine brown sugar, butter and corn syrup; cook over low heat until thick. Pour into an ungreased 13"x9" pan, arranging apple slices on top of syrup. In a mixing bowl, beat eggs, milk and vanilla. Dip French bread in egg mixture and arrange over top of apple slices. Cover and refrigerate overnight. Remove from refrigerator 30 minutes before baking and uncover. Bake at 350 degrees for 35 to 40 minutes, until the top of the bread is golden. Serve French toast with apple slices up and spoon the warm Sauce on top.

Sauce:

1 c. applesauce
10-oz. jar apple jelly
1/2 t. cinnamon
1/8 t. ground cloves

Combine all ingredients in a saucepan and cook over medium heat until jelly is melted.

★ HOT TIP ★ Baked apples are a scrumptious breakfast treat on cozy weekend mornings. Core apples nearly through and place in a greased baking pan. Fill each apple with a teaspoon of honey or maple syrup, a teaspoon of butter and a little cinnamon. Bake at 350 degrees for 35 to 45 minutes, until tender. Serve warm, topped with whipped cream. Fantastic!

Overnight Apple French Toast

Kendall Hale, Lynn, MA

Gingerbread Pancakes

These are oh-so scrumptious topped with tangy Lemon Sauce.

Makes 4 servings

1-1/2 c. all-purpose flour
1 t. baking powder
1/4 t. baking soda
1/4 t. salt
1 t. cinnamon
1/2 t. ground ginger
1-1/4 c. milk
1 egg, beaten
1/4 c. molasses
3 T. oil
Garnish: lemon zest strips

Sift together dry ingredients in a medium bowl; set aside. In a large bowl, beat milk and egg until well blended; stir in molasses and oil. Add flour mixture to milk mixture, stirring just until moistened. Pour batter by 1/3 cupfuls onto a lightly greased hot griddle. Cook over medium heat until bubbly on top; flip and cook until golden. Serve with Lemon Sauce and garnish with lemon zest strips.

Lemon Sauce:

1/2 c. sugar
1 T. cornstarch
1/2 t. nutmeg
1 c. water
2 T. butter
1/2 t. lemon zest
2 T. lemon juice

Stir together sugar, cornstarch and nutmeg in a small saucepan; add water. Cook over medium heat until thick and bubbly; cook and stir 2 more minutes. Remove from heat; add remaining ingredients. Stir just until butter melts. Serve warm.

★ DOUBLE DUTY ★ Don't toss that lemon half after it's been juiced! Wrap it and store in the freezer, ready to grate whenever a recipe calls for fresh lemon zest.

Gingerbread Pancakes

Tamara Ahrens, Sparta, MI

Mom's Everything Waffles

The delicious flavors of peanut butter, pecans, blueberries and even chocolate come together in this one-of-a-kind breakfast favorite.

Serves 4 to 6

2 c. biscuit baking mix
1-1/2 c. quick-cooking oats, uncooked
1/4 c. wheat germ
1/2 c. chopped pecans or walnuts
2 eggs, beaten
1/4 c. peanut butter
1/2 c. vanilla yogurt
3-1/2 c. low-fat milk, divided
1 c. blueberries
Optional: 1/4 c. mini chocolate chips
Garnish: maple syrup, fruit topping, whipped cream

Combine baking mix, oats, wheat germ and nuts in a large bowl; set aside. In a separate bowl, whisk together eggs, peanut butter, yogurt and 3 cups milk. Add to dry ingredients and stir. Add remaining milk as needed to get the consistency of applesauce. Fold in berries and chocolate chips, if desired. Pour by 1/2 cupfuls onto a preheated waffle iron that has been sprayed with non-stick vegetable spray. Bake until crisp, according to manufacturer's directions. Serve with maple syrup or fruit topping and a dollop of whipped cream.

Cris Goode, Mooresville, IN

Peach Oatmeal Pancakes

One morning I mentioned to my three-year-old daughter that I was making pancakes from scratch. She told me, "Mommy, I don't want scratchy pancakes, I just want pancakes!" This recipe will forever be known as "scratchy" peach oatmeal pancakes...which she loves, by the way!

Makes about one dozen pancakes

1 c. quick-cooking oats, uncooked
1/2 c. brown sugar, packed
1 T. cinnamon
2 egg whites, beaten
1 T. vanilla extract
1 peach, peeled, pitted and diced
Optional: 1/2 c. chopped nuts

In a large bowl, combine pancake mix, oats, brown sugar and cinnamon; mix well. Stir in remaining ingredients. Pour batter by 1/4 cupfuls onto a hot buttered griddle. Turn pancakes when bubbles form and start to pop; cook other side until golden.

Mom's Everything Waffles

Jo Ann, Gooseberry Patch

Blueberry-Lemon Crepes

A scrumptious and refreshing breakfast!

Makes 6 servings

3-oz. pkg. cream cheese, softened
1-1/2 c. half-and-half
1 T. lemon juice
3-3/4 pkg. instant lemon pudding mix
1/2 c. biscuit baking mix
1 egg, beaten
6 T. milk
1 c. blueberry pie filling

Combine cream cheese, half-and-half, lemon juice and dry pudding mix in a bowl. Beat with an electric mixer on low speed for 2 minutes. Refrigerate for 30 minutes. Lightly grease a 6" skillet and place over medium-high heat. In a bowl, combine biscuit baking mix, egg and milk. Beat until smooth. Pour 2 tablespoons of batter into skillet for each crepe. Rotating the skillet quickly, allow batter to cover the bottom of the skillet. Cook each crepe until lightly golden, then flip, cooking again until just golden. Spoon 2 tablespoonfuls of cream cheese mixture onto each crepe and roll up. Top with remaining cream cheese mixture and pie filling.

Lynnette Jones, East Flat Rock, NC

Blueberry Buckwheat Pancakes

Buckwheat pancakes just taste like fall! Feel free to use your own favorite fresh or frozen berries.

Makes 4 servings

1-1/2 c. buckwheat flour
1/2 t. baking powder
1/2 t. baking soda
1/4 t. salt
1 c. buttermilk
2 egg whites, beaten
1 egg, beaten
1 T. honey
1 T. canola oil
1 t. vanilla extract
1 c. blueberries, thawed if frozen
Garnish: maple syrup, fresh fruit

In a bowl, mix flour, baking powder, baking soda and salt. In a separate bowl, stir together buttermilk, egg whites, egg, honey, oil and vanilla. Add buttermilk mixture to flour mixture; stir well. Gently fold in blueberries. Heat a lightly greased skillet over medium heat. Add batter by 1/4 cupfuls. Cook until bubbles appear on top, about 1-1/2 minutes. Turn; cook other side until golden, about 1-1/2 minutes. Top with more fresh fruit or maple syrup, as desired.

Blueberry-Lemon Crepes

Vickie, Gooseberry Patch

Nutty Maple Waffles

Crunchy pecans paired with maple...a great way to begin the day! Top with plenty of butter and rich maple syrup.

Makes 8 servings

1-1/2 c. all-purpose flour
2 T. sugar
1 t. baking powder
1/4 t. salt
2 eggs, separated
12-oz. can evaporated milk
3 T. oil
1/2 t. maple extract
1/2 c. pecans, finely chopped

Combine flour, sugar, baking powder and salt in a medium bowl; mix well and set aside. Combine egg yolks, evaporated milk, oil and maple extract in a large bowl; blend well. Gradually add flour mixture, beating well after each addition; set aside. Beat egg whites in a small bowl at high speed with an electric mixer until stiff peaks form; fold into batter. For each waffle, pour 1/2 cup batter onto a preheated, greased waffle iron; sprinkle with one tablespoon nuts. Cook according to manufacturer's instructions.

Cindy Jamieson, Ontario, Canada

Chocolate Chip-Pumpkin Waffles

These taste wonderful, and the kids are none the wiser that they are a tad healthier!

Makes 4 servings

1 egg, beaten
3/4 c. canned pumpkin
1/4 c. brown sugar, packed
1/4 c. butter, melted and slightly cooled
1-3/4 c. milk
1-1/2 c. all-purpose flour
1/2 c. whole-wheat flour
1 T. flax meal
1-1/2 t. pumpkin pie spice
1 T. baking powder
1/2 t. salt
1/2 c. semi-sweet chocolate chips
Optional: vanilla yogurt, cinnamon-sugar, toasted pumpkin seeds

In a bowl, whisk together egg, pumpkin, brown sugar, butter and milk. Add dry ingredients; whisk well until smooth. Fold in chocolate chips. Pour batter by 1/2 cupfuls into a greased hot waffle iron. Cook waffles according to manufacturer's directions. Top waffles with a dollop of yogurt, cinnamon-sugar and pumpkin seeds, if desired.

Nutty Maple Waffles

Bev Ray, Brandon, FL

Overnight Buttermilk-Raisin Pancakes

These pancakes are a breakfast time-saver, so we can enjoy every minute of Christmas morning.

Makes 9 servings

2 c. quick-cooking oats, uncooked
2 c. buttermilk
1/2 c. all-purpose flour
2 T. sugar
1 t. baking powder
1 t. baking soda
1/2 t. cinnamon
1/2 t. salt
2 eggs, beaten
1/4 c. butter, melted
1/2 c. raisins
Optional: chopped walnuts, additional raisins
Garnish: syrup

Mix together oats and buttermilk in a medium bowl; cover and refrigerate overnight. Sift together flour, sugar, baking powder, baking soda, cinnamon and salt in a large bowl. Make a well in the center; add oat mixture, eggs, butter and raisins. Stir just until moistened. Allow batter to stand 20 minutes before cooking. If batter is too thick, add more buttermilk, one tablespoon at a time, until batter reaches desired consistency. Heat a lightly greased large skillet over medium heat. Pour batter by 1/4 cupfuls into skillet. Cook pancakes until bubbles appear on top; flip and cook until golden on both sides. Top with walnuts and additional raisins, if desired, and serve with syrup.

★ FREEZE IT ★ **Extra waffles and pancakes can be frozen in plastic freezer bags for up to a month. Reheat them in a toaster for a hearty, quick weekday breakfast.**

Overnight Buttermilk-Raisin Pancakes

Jo Ann, Gooseberry Patch

Perfect Blueberry Pancakes

Keep pancakes warm & toasty in a 200-degree oven.

Makes one dozen pancakes

1 c. milk
1/2 c. water
1 c. plus 2 T. whole-wheat flour
1/2 c. cornmeal
1 t. baking powder
1/2 t. baking soda
1/4 t. salt
1 c. blueberries
2 T. oil, divided
Garnish: jam or syrup

Mix together milk and water in a small bowl; set aside. Sift together flour, cornmeal, baking powder, baking soda and salt in a large bowl; mix well. Stir in milk mixture just until combined. Fold in blueberries; let stand 5 minutes. Heat one tablespoon oil in a large skillet over medium heat. Pour 1/4 cup batter per pancake into skillet; cook until bubbly on top and edges are slightly dry. Turn and cook other side until golden. Repeat with remaining oil and batter. Serve warm with jam or syrup, as desired.

Becky Hall, Belton, MO

Honey-Cinnamon Pancake Syrup

My family loves to pour on the syrup when eating pancakes, waffles or French toast. This simple recipe is yummy but not so sugary.

Makes 4 servings

1 c. water
1 c. honey
1 t. cinnamon
1/8 t. orange zest
1/8 t. lemon zest

Combine all ingredients in a small saucepan over medium heat. Bring to a boil; reduce heat to low. Simmer, uncovered, for about 30 minutes, stirring often. Serve warm.

★ GIFT IT ★ Been invited to a weekend brunch? A vintage canning jar filled with Honey-Cinnamon Pancake Syrup makes a thoughtful hostess gift. Tie on a topper of colorful fabric with raffia.

Perfect Blueberry Pancakes

Marion Sundberg, Yorba Linda, CA

Florence's Buttermilk Pancakes

My mother's recipe...fluffy, light and yummy! I like to create animals and other shapes with the batter...you'll get about 2 dozen small pancakes.

Makes 6 servings

1 c. all-purpose flour
1 t. sugar
1 t. baking soda
1 t. baking powder
1 t. salt
1 c. buttermilk
1 egg, beaten
2 T. oil
Garnish: maple syrup

Mix together dry ingredients; add wet ingredients except syrup and mix well. Ladle 1/4 cupfuls of batter onto a hot, greased griddle and cook on one side until bubbles appear all over pancakes. Flip and continue cooking until golden on both sides. Serve hot with maple syrup.

Cindy Williams, Owensboro, KY

Luscious Blueberry Syrup

So quick & easy! It's delicious drizzled warm or cold over waffles, pancakes and even over ice cream or a slice of pound cake.

Makes about 2-1/2 cups

1/2 c. sugar
1 T. cornstarch
1/3 c. water
2 c. fresh or frozen blueberries

In a saucepan over medium heat, combine sugar and cornstarch. Stir in water gradually. Add berries; bring to a boil. Boil, stirring constantly, for one minute, or until mixture thickens. Serve warm, or pour into a covered jar and keep in the refrigerator for several days.

★ TAKE IT TO GO ★ A lasting memory of the fun...send brunch guests home with a jar of homemade syrup or a new sugar shaker to add to their baking collections.

Florence's Buttermilk Pancakes

Jennifer Yandle, Indian Trail, NC

Make-Ahead Pumpkin Pie French Toast

It's a great Sunday morning breakfast...it can bake while you get ready for church. It's also super-easy for husbands to whip up so Mom can sleep in just a bit on Saturday morning!

Makes 8 servings

1 loaf French, Italian, challah or
   Hawaiian bread, cut into 1-inch
   slices
3 eggs, beaten
1-1/2 c. milk
1 c. half-and-half
1/2 c. egg substitute
1 T. pumpkin pie spice
1 t. vanilla extract
1/4 t. salt
1/2 c. brown sugar, packed
1 to 2 T. butter, sliced

Arrange bread slices in bottom of a greased 13"x9" baking pan. Whisk together eggs, milk, half-and-half, egg substitute, spice, vanilla and salt. Stir in brown sugar; pour mixture over bread slices. Refrigerate, covered, overnight. Dot top with butter and bake, uncovered, at 350 degrees for 40 to 45 minutes.

Mardell Lamb, Pavilion, NY

Mulled Cider Syrup

This delicious, spicy pancake & waffle syrup has been a family favorite for many years now. The apple jelly thickens it.

Makes about 1-1/2 cups

2 c. apple cider
1/4 c. brown sugar, packed
1/4 c. sugar
1/2 c. apple jelly
1/2 t. cinnamon
1/4 t. ground cloves
1/4 t. nutmeg

In a one-quart saucepan over medium heat, combine cider and sugars. Cook over low heat without stirring until sugars dissolve. Stir in apple jelly and spices. Heat to boiling over medium heat. Reduce heat to low; simmer and stir until jelly melts. Remove from heat; cool slightly. Serve warm, or cover and refrigerate until ready to use. Reheat until warm if refrigerated.

Make-Ahead Pumpkin Pie French Toast

Kris Coburn, Dansville, NY

Strawberry Cheesecake French Toast

Two favorite foods in one dish... strawberries and cheesecake. Now that's something to wake up to!

Makes 4 servings

1/2 c. cream cheese, softened
2 T. powdered sugar
2 T. strawberry preserves
8 slices country white bread
2 eggs
1/2 c. half-and-half
2 T. sugar
4 T. butter, divided

Combine cream cheese and powdered sugar in a small bowl; mix well. Stir in preserves. Spread cream cheese mixture evenly over 4 slices of bread; top with remaining slices to form sandwiches. Whisk together eggs, half-and-half and sugar in a medium bowl; set aside. Melt 2 tablespoons butter in a large skillet over medium heat. Dip each sandwich into egg mixture, completely covering both sides. Cook 2 sandwiches at a time for one to 2 minutes per side, or until golden. Melt remaining butter and cook remaining sandwiches as instructed.

Ashlee Haefs, Buna, TX

Red Velvet Pancakes

Red velvet cake is one of my family's favorites, so with this recipe we can have it for breakfast...what a great way to start the day!

Makes one dozen pancakes

1-1/2 c. all-purpose flour
2 T. baking cocoa
4 t. sugar
1-1/2 t. baking powder
1/2 t. baking soda
1 t. cinnamon
1 t. salt
2 eggs
1-1/4 c. buttermilk
1 T. red food coloring
1-1/2 t. vanilla extract
1/4 c. butter, melted
Garnish: maple syrup, butter,
   whipped cream cheese

In a bowl, whisk together all dry ingredients. In a separate bowl, mix eggs, buttermilk, food coloring and vanilla. Add to dry ingredients and mix well. Fold in melted butter. Using an ice cream scoop, drop batter onto a lightly greased, hot griddle and cook until edges darken, about 5 minutes. Flip and cook until done. Serve topped with syrup and butter or whipped cream cheese.

Strawberry Cheesecake French Toast

Virginia Watson, Scranton, PA

Chicken & Waffles

Such a funny combination...but it's really tasty, so give it a try!

Makes 4 servings

3 lbs. chicken
salt and pepper to taste
2 to 4 T. olive oil
2 14-1/2 oz. cans chicken broth
1 stalk celery, chopped
1 carrot, peeled and chopped
1 onion, chopped
1 bay leaf
3 T. all-purpose flour
1/4 c. cold water

Sprinkle chicken with salt and pepper. Heat oil in a large deep skillet over medium-high heat. Add chicken to skillet; cook on all sides until golden. Add broth, vegetables and bay leaf to skillet. Reduce heat to low; cover and simmer until chicken is tender, about one hour. Remove chicken, reserving broth in skillet.

Cool chicken and tear into bite-size pieces. Skim fat from reserved broth; bring broth to a boil. Shake together flour and water in a small jar until smooth. Add flour mixture gradually to skillet, stirring constantly. Continue to cook until gravy is thickened. Return chicken to skillet; keep warm over low heat. Serve chicken and gravy over Golden Waffles.

Golden Waffles:

2 c. biscuit baking mix
1-1/3 c. milk
1 egg, beaten
2 T. oil
Optional: 1/2 t. poultry seasoning

Stir together all ingredients until blended. Pour batter by 1/2 cupfuls onto a preheated, lightly greased waffle iron. Bake waffles according to manufacturer's directions.

★ VARIETY FOR FUN ★ Breakfast for dinner is a fun and frugal treat! Enjoy waffles, French toast and pancakes in the evening, when there's more time to cook. Add a yummy fruit salad and a side of sausage or bacon, if you like.

Chicken & Waffles

Jill Velentine, Jackson, TN

Baked Pancakes with Sausage

I cook up the sausage and mix the dry ingredients the night before to save time in the morning!

Serves 8 to 10

1-3/4 c. all-purpose flour
4 t. baking powder
5 t. sugar
1 t. salt
3 eggs
1-1/2 c. milk
3 T. margarine, melted
1 lb. pork sausage breakfast links, browned and drained
Garnish: butter, warm syrup

Mix together flour, baking powder, sugar and salt; set aside. In a large bowl, beat eggs until fluffy; mix in milk and margarine. Gradually stir in flour mixture until smooth. Pour batter into a greased 15"x10" jelly-roll pan. Arrange sausages on top of batter. Bake at 450 degrees for 15 minutes, or until pancakes are done. Cut into squares and serve with butter and syrup.

Joseph Drushal, Chicago, IL

Bacon Griddle Cakes

So simple but so delicious! Why didn't I think of this sooner?

Serves 4 to 6

12 slices bacon
2 c. pancake mix
Garnish: butter, maple syrup

On a griddle set to medium heat, cook bacon until crisp. Drain, reserving 2 tablespoons drippings. Meanwhile, prepare pancake mix according to package directions, omitting a little of the water or milk for a thicker batter. Arrange bacon slices 2 inches apart on griddle greased with reserved drippings. Slowly pour pancake batter over each piece of bacon, covering each slice. Cook until golden on both sides; serve with butter and maple syrup.

★ FREEZE IT ★ If you're cooking up bacon, why not cook up the whole package? Cooked bacon can easily be frozen. Wrap individual portions in paper towels to cushion, then place the towel-wrapped portions into plastic zipping bags. Freeze and store for up to six weeks.

Baked Pancakes with Sausage

Gingered Kiwi Fruit, Page 166

CHAPTER FIVE

Breakfast Sides

Mini Hashbrown Casseroles, Page 178

Hearty Hashbrowns, Page 170

Patricia Tilley, Sabine, WV

Oven-Fried Bacon Potatoes

Sprinkle with a little shredded Cheddar cheese if you like...tasty!

Serves 6 to 8

3 T. butter, melted
1-1/2 lb. redskin potatoes, cut into
   1/4-inch slices
1/4 t. salt
1/4 t. pepper
6 slices bacon
Garnish: fresh thyme leaves

Coat a cast-iron skillet with melted butter. Layer potatoes in skillet; season each layer with salt and pepper. Arrange uncooked bacon slices on top. Bake, uncovered, at 425 degrees for 40 minutes, or until bacon is crisp and potatoes are tender. Garnish with thyme leaves.

Hope Davenport, Portland, TX

Ham & Ranch Potatoes

My family loves this dish and it's so easy to make. The dressing mix gives it a wonderful flavor.

Makes 6 servings

2 lbs. redskin potatoes, peeled and
   quartered
8-oz. pkg. cream cheese, softened
1-oz. pkg. buttermilk ranch salad
   dressing mix
10-3/4 oz. can cream of potato soup
16-oz. pkg. cooked ham, cubed
1 c. shredded Cheddar cheese
salt and pepper to taste

Place potatoes in a slow cooker. Combine cream cheese and dressing mix; add soup and mix well. Add cream cheese mixture to slow cooker and mix with potatoes. Cover and cook on low setting for 6-1/2 hours. Stir in ham and top with cheese; add salt and pepper to taste. Cover and cook for another 15 to 30 minutes, until cheese is melted.

Oven-Fried Bacon Potatoes

Joanna Watson-Donahue,

Lubbock, TX

Sausage Balls

My mom and I have made this tasty recipe for many family gatherings, including the morning after my wedding. It's so simple and uses only three ingredients.

Makes 3 to 4 dozen

16-oz. pkg. ground pork breakfast
   sausage
16-oz. pkg. shredded sharp Cheddar,
   Pepper Jack or mozzarella cheese
1 c. all-purpose flour

Combine all ingredients in a large bowl. Knead together until completely blended. Form mixture into one to 1-1/2 inch balls. Place balls one inch apart on parchment paper-lined baking sheets. Bake at 350 degrees for 15 to 20 minutes, until golden and and sausage is no longer pink. Cool slightly before serving. May be baked and refrigerated up to one week in a plastic zipping bag and warmed at serving time.

★ SAVVY SIDE ★ **Sausage Balls are perfect little bites alongside your favorite breakfast eggs. They are also a great choice for a brunch buffet spread. Set out a tray of these tasty morsels with some dipping sauces like mustard, catsup or ranch dressing.**

Sausage Balls

Becky Woods, Ballwin, MO

Smoked Gouda Grits

These smoky and creamy grits are the perfect addition to scrambled eggs and breakfast sausage...yum!

Serves 6 to 8

6 c. chicken broth
2 c. milk
1 t. salt
1/2 t. white pepper
2 c. quick-cooking grits, uncooked
1-2/3 c. shredded smoked Gouda
    cheese
3 T. butter, softened

Bring broth, milk, salt and pepper to a boil in a large saucepan over medium heat. Gradually whisk in grits. Reduce heat; cover and simmer, stirring occasionally, about 5 minutes or until thickened. Add cheese and butter; stir until melted.

★ TIME-SAVING SHORTCUT ★
Save a little time by buying frozen diced potatoes with peppers & onions already added in. All the flavor with less work!

Vickie, Gooseberry Patch

Mexicali Breakfast Potatoes

This hearty potato dish is a wonderful change from ordinary hashbrowns! It's become a tailgating brunch favorite for our family & friends. Garnish with sour cream and a sprinkle of cheese.

Makes 8 servings

32-oz. pkg. frozen diced potatoes
1/4 c. onion, diced
1/4 c. red pepper, diced
1/4 c. canned diced green chiles
1 T. Dijon mustard
1-1/4 t. ground cumin
1-1/4 t. salt
1 t. pepper
1/2 t. cayenne pepper
1 T. canola oil

In a large bowl, combine all ingredients except oil; mix well and set aside. Add oil to a large skillet; heat over medium heat. Add potato mixture to skillet. Cook, stirring often, for 12 to 15 minutes, until potatoes are golden.

Smoked Gouda Grits

Donna West, Spring Creek, NV

Golden Potato Pancakes

A real old-time comfort food, good for either breakfast or dinner.

Makes 4 pancakes

2 c. mashed potatoes
1 egg, beaten
6 to 8 saltine crackers, crushed
salt and pepper to taste
oil or bacon drippings for frying

Mix together potatoes, egg and cracker crumbs; add salt and pepper to taste. Let stand for a few minutes. Heat oil or drippings in a skillet over medium heat; drop potato mixture by large spoonfuls into skillet. Cook until golden on one side; flip over and cook until golden on other side.

Pam Massey, Marshall, AR

Krunchy Krispies Bacon

Just a little country trick to make the same old thing taste a little different... adds a little extra crunch.

Makes 6 servings

12 slices bacon, halved
1/2 c. all-purpose flour

Roll bacon slices in flour, shaking off any excess flour. Arrange bacon on an aluminum foil-lined baking sheet. Bake at 375 degrees until bacon is crisp, about 12 to 15 minutes depending on thickness of bacon. Drain on paper towels before serving.

★ HOT TIP ★ A quick, no-mess way to cook bacon. Arrange bacon slices on a broiler pan and place the pan 3 to 4 inches from the preheated broiler. Broil for one to 2 minutes on each side, depending on how crispy you like your bacon.

Golden Potato Pancakes

Dylan Bradshaw, Los Angeles, CA

Escalloped Apples

An old-fashioned dish that goes great with any meal!

Makes 6 servings

1/2 c. butter
2 c. fresh bread crumbs
5 tart apples, peeled, cored and
   sliced
1/2 c. sugar
1/2 t. cinnamon
1/4 t. ground cloves

Melt butter in a saucepan. Add bread crumbs and toast lightly for about 2 minutes; set aside. Toss apples with sugar, cinnamon and cloves. In a greased 8"x8" baking pan, layer half of the apples and half of the toasted bread crumbs. Repeat with the remaining apples and bread crumbs. Bake at 325 degrees, covered, for 45 minutes or until apples are tender. Bake uncovered 15 more minutes.

Marilyn Epley, Stillwater, OK

Honeyed Fruit & Rice

Jasmine rice is also known as fragrant rice and can be found in many markets or specialty stores.

Makes 2 servings

2 c. cooked jasmine rice
1/3 c. dried cranberries
1/3 c. dried apricots, chopped
1/4 c. honey
Garnish: milk

Stir together hot cooked rice, cranberries, apricots and honey. Divide into 2 bowls; top with milk.

★ FLAVOR BURST ★ **Add a delicious crunch to Honeyed Fruit & Rice...just add 1/4 cup slivered, toasted almonds or walnuts.**

Escalloped Apples

Zoe Bennett, Columbia, SC

Sweet & Spicy Bacon

Try this easy-to-fix bacon at your next brunch...guests will love it!

Serves 4 to 5

1/2 c. brown sugar, packed
2 T. chili powder
1 t. ground cumin
1 t. cumin seed
1 t. ground coriander
1/4 t. cayenne pepper
10 thick slices bacon

Line a 15"x10" jelly-roll pan with aluminum foil. Place a wire rack on pan and set aside. Combine all ingredients except bacon. Sprinkle mixture onto a large piece of wax paper. Press bacon slices into mixture, turning to coat well. Arrange in a single layer on wire rack in pan; place pan on center rack of oven. Bake at 400 degrees for 12 minutes; turn bacon over. Bake for 10 more minutes, or until deep brown but not burned. Drain on paper towels; serve warm.

★ KID FRIENDLY ★ Breakfast sliders! Whip up your favorite pancake batter and make silver dollar-size pancakes. Sandwich them together with slices of Sweet & Spicy Bacon. Serve with maple syrup on the side for dipping...yum!

Sweet & Spicy Bacon

Cindy Coffman, Lewisberry, PA

Hidden Pear Salad

This classic fruity salad is
so refreshing.

Serves 6 to 8

16-oz. can pears, drained and
   juice reserved
3-oz. pkg. lime gelatin mix
3-oz. pkg. cream cheese, softened
1/4 t. lemon juice
1.3-oz. pkg. whipped topping mix
Garnish: additional whipped
   topping, lime slices

Pour pear juice into a saucepan;
bring to a boil over medium heat.
Remove from heat; stir in gelatin
mix until dissolved. Set aside to cool
to room temperature. Purée pears in
a blender; set aside. Blend cream
cheese and lemon juice until light
and fluffy; mix in pears and set aside.
Prepare whipped topping according
to package directions; fold into pear
mixture. Add cooled gelatin; pour
into an 8"x8" baking pan, and chill
overnight. Garnish with whipped
topping and lime slices, as desired.

★ SAVVY SECRET ★ Juicy fresh pears are
one of fall's delights. Green Anjou pears and
sandy-colored Bosc will hold their shape nicely
when cooked, while red or yellow Bartlett pears
are delicious for eating out of hand.

Hidden Pear Salad

Sharon Demers, Dolores, CO

Gingered Kiwi Fruit

This very refreshing, colorful salad is delightful to take to bridal and baby showers.

Makes 4 servings

3 T. sugar
3 T. water
2 T. crystallized ginger, minced
1/4 t. vanilla extract
4 kiwi fruit, peeled and sliced
2 oranges, peeled and sliced

In a small saucepan over medium-high heat, combine sugar, water and ginger. Bring to a boil. Stirring constantly, boil until mixture reaches a light syrup consistency, about 3 minutes. Remove from heat and stir in vanilla. Cool slightly. In a dessert dish, gently stir fruit slices and ginger syrup until well mixed. Cover and refrigerate until well chilled, about 2 hours.

★ TIME-SAVING SHORTCUT ★
Peel kiwi fruit in a jiffy. Slice off both ends, then stand the kiwi on one end and slice off strips of peel from top to bottom.

Marcia Shaffer, Conneaut Lake, PA

Garden Tomato Rarebit

Spoon this cheesy, creamy dish over thick slices of country-style bread... yummy morning, noon or night!

Makes 6 servings

2 T. butter
2 T. all-purpose flour
1 c. light cream, warmed
1/8 t. baking soda
1/2 c. tomatoes, finely chopped
2 c. shredded Cheddar cheese
2 eggs, lightly beaten
1 t. dry mustard
fresh basil to taste, chopped
cayenne pepper, salt and pepper
  to taste
6 slices bread, toasted

In a saucepan over medium heat, melt butter. Stir in flour; cook and stir 2 to 3 minutes. Slowly pour in cream; cook and stir until mixture thickens. In a small bowl, stir baking soda into tomatoes. Add tomato mixture to saucepan with remaining ingredients except toast. Reduce heat to low; cook and stir until cheese melts. Do not boil. To serve, spoon over slices of toast.

Gingered Kiwi Fruit

Debi Gilpin, Bluefield, WV

Grits Au Gratin

Quick and versatile, this side is great for breakfast, lunch or dinner.

Makes 4 servings

3 c. water
3/4 c. quick-cooking grits, uncooked
1 t. salt
1/4 lb. sharp Cheddar cheese, thinly
  sliced
1/2 c. milk
1/2 c. dry bread crumbs
1 T. butter, melted
1/4 t. paprika

Bring 3 cups water to a boil in a saucepan over medium heat; stir in grits and salt. Cook 3 to 5 minutes; remove from heat. Alternate layers of grits and cheese in a greased 1-1/2 quart casserole dish; pour milk over the top. Toss bread crumbs and butter in a bowl; sprinkle over casserole. Sprinkle with paprika; bake, uncovered, at 325 degrees for 20 to 25 minutes.

Becky Drees, Pittsfield, MA

Autumn Sweet Potato Hash

A delightfully different side to serve with creamy scrambled eggs and hot buttered toast.

Serves 6 to 8

3 T. olive oil
2 c. sweet potatoes, peeled and diced
2 c. butternut squash, peeled and
  diced
1/2 c. red pepper, diced
1/2 c. green pepper, diced
1/2 c. onion, diced
1/2 t. garlic, minced
1/4 c. fresh sage, thinly sliced
1/4 t. salt
1/4 t. white pepper
1/2 c. vegetable broth

In an oven-proof sauté pan over medium heat, combine oil, sweet potatoes, squash, peppers and onion. Sauté until vegetables begin to soften and turn golden. Add garlic, sage, salt and pepper; continue to sauté for one minute. Stir in broth. Bake, uncovered, at 350 degrees just until vegetables are tender, about 10 to 15 minutes. A little more broth may be added to keep hash from drying out.

Grits Au Gratin

Stephanie Mayer, Portsmouth, VA

Hearty Hashbrowns

Use leftover cooked potatoes from dinner for a speedy start.

Serves 6 to 8

8 slices bacon, crisply cooked,
    crumbled and drippings reserved
10 c. potatoes, peeled, cooked and
    cubed
3 onions, sliced
salt and pepper to taste

In a large skillet, heat reserved drippings over medium heat. Add potatoes and onions to skillet. Cook until potatoes are golden and onions are tender, about 25 minutes. Add salt and pepper to taste; stir in reserved bacon.

Bev Fisher, Mesa, AZ

Tomato Salad with Grilled Bread

I found this unusual recipe and then tweaked it to make it my own. It's great for backyard barbecues. I guarantee you'll like it, too!

Makes 6 servings

3 lbs. tomatoes, cut into chunks
1 cucumber, peeled and sliced
4-oz. container crumbled feta cheese
1/4 c. balsamic vinegar
1/4 t. salt
1/4 t. pepper
8 thick slices crusty Italian bread,
    cubed
2 c. watermelon, cut into 1/2-inch
    cubes
1 red onion, very thinly sliced and
    separated into rings
3.8-oz. can sliced black olives, drained
1/4 c. plus 1/2 t. olive oil
1/2 c. fresh basil, torn

Combine tomatoes, cucumber, cheese, vinegar, salt and pepper in a large serving bowl. Toss to mix; cover and chill one hour. Place bread cubes on an ungreased baking sheet. Bake at 350 degrees for 5 minutes, or until lightly golden. At serving time, add bread cubes and remaining ingredients to tomato mixture. Toss very lightly and serve.

Hearty Hashbrowns

Lori Rosenberg,
University Heights, OH

Spring Ramen Salad

This yummy recipe is truly made to clean out the fridge...you can put almost anything in it!

Makes 4 servings

3-oz. pkg. chicken-flavored ramen
  noodles
1 t. sesame oil
1/2 c. seedless grapes, halved
1/2 c. apple, cored and diced
1/4 c. pineapple, diced
2 green onions, diced
1 c. cooked chicken, cubed
1 c. Muenster cheese, cubed
1-1/2 T. lemon juice
1/8 c. canola oil
1 t. sugar
Garnish: sesame seed

Set aside seasoning packet from ramen noodles. Cook noodles according to package directions. Drain noodles; rinse with cold water. In a bowl, toss sesame oil with noodles to coat. Stir in fruit, onions, chicken and cheese. In a separate bowl, whisk together lemon juice, canola oil, sugar and 1/2 teaspoon of contents of seasoning packet. Pour over noodle mixture; toss to coat. Garnish with sesame seed. Cover and chill before serving.

★ FLAVOR BURST ★ Toasting really brings out the flavor of sesame seed and chopped nuts...and it's simple. Add seeds or nuts to a small dry skillet. Cook and stir over low heat for a few minutes, until toasty and golden.

Spring Ramen Salad

Megan Brooks, Antioch, TN

Diner-Style Corned Beef Hash

Top each portion with an egg... sunny-side up, of course!

Makes 2 servings

1 T. oil
2 potatoes, peeled and diced
1 onion, chopped
12-oz. can corned beef, chopped
1 t. pepper
2-1/2 T. cider vinegar, divided

Heat oil in a skillet over medium-high heat. Add potatoes and onion; sauté until light golden. Stir in corned beef, pepper and one tablespoon vinegar. Cook for 3 to 5 minutes; stir in remaining vinegar. Partially cover skillet. Reduce heat and cook for about 20 minutes, stirring occasionally, until potatoes are tender.

Kathy Arner, Phoenix, AZ

Cheddar-Chile Brunch Potatoes

This recipe came to me years ago from the school where I work...it is requested every time we have a staff breakfast. It's easy to make and can be made the night before. I have served it at church brunches too and there's never any leftovers. My family pouts when they know the whole pan goes with me, so I have to make two pans!

Makes 12 servings

1-lb. pkg. ground pork sausage,
   browned and drained
16-oz. container light sour cream
10-3/4 oz. can cream of chicken soup
7-oz. can diced mild green chiles
8-oz. pkg. shredded Cheddar cheese
30-oz. pkg. frozen shredded
   hashbrowns, thawed
30-oz. pkg. frozen spicy or western
   shredded hashbrowns, thawed

Mix all ingredients except hashbrowns in a large bowl; stir until well mixed. Add hashbrowns and stir until coated well. Transfer to a greased 15"x11" baking pan. Bake, uncovered, at 375 degrees for one hour, or until deep golden. Let stand for 5 minutes before serving.

Diner-Style Corned Beef Hash

Virginia Watson, Scranton, PA

Pennsylvania Dutch Scrapple

Squares of this savory dish are usually served for breakfast...but sometimes, it's great for dinner too.

Makes 12 servings

1 lb. boneless pork loin, chopped
1 c. cornmeal
14-1/2 oz. can chicken broth
1/4 t. dried thyme
1/4 t. salt
1/2 c. all-purpose flour
1/4 t. pepper
2 T. oil
Optional: maple syrup

In a saucepan, cover pork with water; bring to a boil over medium heat. Simmer until fork-tender, about an hour; drain. Process in a food processor until minced. In a large saucepan over medium heat, combine pork, cornmeal, broth, thyme and salt; bring to a boil. Reduce heat and simmer, stirring constantly, for 2 minutes, or until mixture is very thick. Line a 9"x5" loaf pan with wax paper, letting paper extend above top of pan. Spoon pork mixture into pan; cover and chill for 4 hours to overnight. Unmold; cut into slices and set aside. On a plate, combine flour and pepper. Coat slices with flour mixture. In a large skillet, heat oil over medium heat; cook slices on both sides until golden. Drizzle with syrup, if desired.

★ SAVVY SIDE ★ Serve this breakfast side dish with sweet or savory dips including catsup, mustard, grape jelly, applesauce, honey or maple syrup. Mix it with scrambled eggs or even serve it between two slices of bread.

Pennsylvania Dutch Scrapple

Wendy Jacobs, Idaho Falls, ID

Mini Hashbrown Casseroles

Portioned just right to grab & go in the morning...perfect for brunch buffets too.

Makes one to 1-1/2 dozen

16-oz. pkg. ground pork breakfast
   sausage
1/2 c. green pepper, diced
4 eggs
1/2 c. milk
1/2 t. pepper
20-oz. pkg. refrigerated shredded
   hashbrowns
3 T. butter, melted and slightly cooled
1 c. shredded Cheddar cheese

Brown sausage with green pepper in a skillet over medium heat; drain well. Meanwhile, whisk together eggs, milk and pepper in a large bowl. Add sausage mixture and remaining ingredients; mix well. Spoon mixture into lightly greased muffin cups, filling 2/3 full. Bake at 350 degrees for 25 to 30 minutes, until eggs are set and a toothpick inserted in the center tests clean.

★ DOUBLE DUTY ★ Mini Hashbrown Casseroles are not only perfect for brunch buffets, they are great bite-sized appetizers for your game-day spread too!

Mini Hashbrown Casseroles

Beth Kramer, Port Saint Lucie, FL

Strawberry-Hazelnut Grits

This combination of strawberry, cocoa and hazelnut is just too yummy to pass up!

Makes 2 servings

3/4 c. quick-cooking grits, uncooked
1 T. butter
3 T. chocolate-hazelnut spread
6 to 7 strawberries, hulled and
    chopped

Prepare grits according to package directions. Stir in butter and chocolate-hazelnut spread. Fold in strawberries.

Carrie Fostor, Baltic, OH

Kids' Favorite Fruit Salad

This simple recipe will have the kids asking for more! Great for picnics, potlucks and school lunches. I keep it on hand for snacks!

Serves 6 to 8

14-1/2 oz. can peach pie filling
1 c. pineapple, peeled and diced
1 c. seedless red grapes
2 bananas, sliced
11-oz. can mandarin oranges, drained
1 c. mini marshmallows

Mix all ingredients together in a large bowl and refrigerate until chilled.

★ KID FRIENDLY ★ Kids' Favorite Fruit Salad makes a wonderful topping for ice cream, pancakes, waffles and pound cake.

Strawberry-Hazelnut Grits

Double Toffee Coffee Cake, Page 212

CHAPTER SIX

Pastries & Sweet Breads

Pecan Pie Muffins, Page 198

Jumbo Cinnamon Rolls, Page 210

Susan Rogers, Mohnton, PA

Gran-Gran's Sweet Bread

As a child, I always looked forward to my grandmother bringing a loaf of her sweet bread every Easter and Christmas. She didn't use a written recipe, so one time I asked her how she made it, and I wrote it down. It took me several tries until I felt it was as good as Gran-Gran's bread. Thank you, Gran!

Makes 6 loaves

1/2 c. butter, softened
1/2 c. shortening
2-1/4 c. sugar, divided
3 eggs, beaten
2 t. vanilla extract
2 envs. active dry yeast
1 c. warm water
8 c. all-purpose flour
1/2 t. salt
2 c. warm milk
16-oz. pkg. raisins
1/2 c. butter, melted

Blend together butter and shortening in a very large bowl. Gradually add 2 cups sugar, eggs and vanilla, beating well after each addition. Combine yeast and warm water (110 to 115 degrees) in a cup; let stand 5 minutes. Whisk together flour and salt. With a large wooden spoon, gradually stir flour and salt into butter mixture alternately with yeast mixture and warm milk. Mix well; stir in raisins. Turn dough out onto a floured surface. Knead, adding additional flour until dough is smooth and elastic. Return dough to bowl. Lightly spray dough with non-stick vegetable spray; cover with wax paper and a tea towel. Let rise 6 to 8 hours or overnight, until double in bulk. Punch down; divide into 6 equal portions and place in 6 greased 9"x5" loaf pans. Cover and let rise again until rounded, 4 to 6 hours. Drizzle melted butter over loaves; sprinkle each loaf with 2 teaspoons remaining sugar. Bake at 350 degrees for 30 minutes, or until a toothpick inserted in center comes out clean. Cool on wire racks.

Gran-Gran's Sweet Bread

Beth Kramer, Port St. Lucie, FL

Orange Coffee Rolls

The taste of the tropics! For a finishing touch, sprinkle the glaze with orange zest.

Makes 2 dozen

1 env. active dry yeast
1/4 c. warm water
1 c. sugar, divided
2 eggs, beaten
1/2 c. sour cream
1/4 c. plus 2 T. butter, melted and
    divided
1 t. salt
2-3/4 to 3 c. all-purpose flour
1 c. flaked coconut, toasted and
    divided
2 T. orange zest

Combine yeast and warm water (110 to 115 degrees) in a large bowl; let stand 5 minutes. Add 1/4 cup sugar, eggs, sour cream, 1/4 cup butter and salt; beat at medium speed with an electric mixer until blended. Gradually stir in enough flour to make a soft dough. Turn dough out onto a well-floured surface; knead until smooth and elastic (about 5 minutes). Place in a well-greased bowl, turning to grease top. Cover and let rise in a warm place (85 degrees), free from drafts, 1-1/2 hours or until double in bulk.

Punch dough down and divide in half. Roll one portion of dough into a 12-inch circle; brush with one tablespoon melted butter. Combine remaining sugar, coconut and orange zest; sprinkle half of coconut mixture over dough. Cut into 12 wedges; roll up each wedge, beginning at wide end. Place in a greased 13"x9" baking pan, point side down. Repeat with remaining dough, butter and coconut mixture. Cover and let rise in a warm place, free from drafts, 45 minutes or until doubled in bulk. Bake at 350 degrees for 25 to 30 minutes, until golden. (Cover with aluminum foil after 15 minutes to prevent excessive browning, if necessary.) Spoon warm Glaze over warm rolls; sprinkle with remaining coconut.

Glaze:

3/4 c. sugar
1/2 c. sour cream
1/4 c. butter
2 t. orange juice

Combine all ingredients in a small saucepan; bring to a boil. Boil 3 minutes, stirring occasionally. Let cool slightly. Makes 1-1/3 cups.

Orange Coffee Rolls

Tina Stidam, Delaware, OH

Tina's Ooey-Gooey Cinnamon Rolls

Use butter-flavored cooking spray when greasing pans used for baking sweets and confections.

Makes one dozen

1/2 c. water
2 envs. active dry yeast
1 c. buttermilk
1/2 c. plus 3 T. sugar, divided
1 T. salt
4 c. all-purpose flour
4 egg yolks
1-1/2 c. butter, softened and divided
1 T. cinnamon
Optional: 3/4 c. raisins

Heat 1/2 cup water until very warm, about 110 to 115 degrees. Dissolve yeast in very warm water in a large bowl. Add buttermilk, 3 tablespoons sugar, salt, flour, egg yolks and one cup butter. Beat with an electric mixer at high speed 8 minutes, or until smooth. Turn out onto an ungreased baking sheet; cover and refrigerate 6 hours. Roll out dough on a floured surface to a 24-inch by 10-inch rectangle (about 1/2-inch to 3/4-inch thick); melt remaining butter and brush over dough. Combine remaining sugar and cinnamon; mix well and sprinkle over dough. Spread raisins over top, if using; roll up dough jelly-roll style, starting at long edge. Place seam-side down and cut into 2-inch slices. Place on a greased 11"x9" baking sheet; cover and let rise until double in bulk. Bake at 350 degrees for 20 to 25 minutes. Spread Vanilla Glaze over warm rolls.

Vanilla Glaze:

1 vanilla bean
2-3/4 c. powdered sugar
1/2 c. butter, melted
2 T. water
1 T. vanilla extract

Cut vanilla bean in half lengthwise; scrape out seeds from both halves. Combine vanilla bean seeds, powdered sugar, butter, water and vanilla extract in a large bowl and mix until smooth. Makes about 2-1/2 cups.

★ SAVVY SECRET ★ **A convenient place to let yeast dough rise is inside your microwave. Heat a mug of water on high for 2 minutes. Then remove the mug, place the covered bowl of dough inside and close the door.**

Tina's Ooey-Gooey Cinnamon Rolls

Amy Hansen, Louisville, KY

Mother's Rolls

Growing up, we couldn't wait until Mother's rolls were out of the oven and ready to enjoy. Now that I have a family of my own, my children can hardly wait for them to be cool enough to eat!

Makes 15 rolls

1 env. active dry yeast
3/4 c. warm water
3-1/2 c. biscuit baking mix, divided
1 T. sugar
1/4 c. butter, melted
Garnish: additional melted butter

Dissolve yeast in warm water (110 to 115 degrees); let stand 5 minutes. Place 2-1/2 cups biscuit mix in a large bowl; stir in sugar. Add yeast mixture, stirring vigorously. Sprinkle work surface generously with remaining biscuit mix. Place dough on surface and knead 15 to 20 times. Shape heaping tablespoons of dough into balls; arrange on a lightly greased baking sheet. Cover dough with a damp tea towel; set aside in a warm place to rise, about one hour. Brush rolls with melted butter. Bake at 400 degrees for 12 to 15 minutes, until golden. Remove rolls from oven; brush again with melted butter while hot.

Lynda Robson, Boston, MA

Cherry Turnovers

These are so quick & easy but taste like you spent hours in the kitchen making them!

Makes 8 turnovers

17-1/4 oz. pkg. frozen puff pastry, thawed
21-oz. can cherry pie filling, drained
1 c. powdered sugar
2 T. water

Separate puff pastry sheets and cut each into 4 squares. Divide pie filling evenly among squares. Brush pastry edges with water and fold in half diagonally. Seal and crimp edges with a fork. With a knife, make a small slit in tops of turnovers to vent. Bake on an ungreased baking sheet at 400 degrees for 15 to 18 minutes, until puffed and golden. Let cool slightly. Blend together powdered sugar and water; drizzle over warm turnovers.

Mother's Rolls

Emily Oravecz, New York, NY

Potato Doughnuts

What's better than a warm doughnut and a hot cup of coffee? These are also a great way to use up leftover mashed potatoes.

Makes 4 dozen

2 envs. active dry yeast
1/2 c. warm water
1 c. sugar
3/4 c. shortening
1-1/2 c. mashed potatoes
3 eggs, beaten
2 c. milk
1 T. salt
1 T. lemon extract
6 to 8 c. all-purpose flour
oil for frying
Garnish: cinnamon-sugar, powdered
   sugar

Dissolve yeast in very warm water, 110 to 115 degrees; set aside. In a separate bowl, blend together sugar and shortening. Add potatoes, eggs, milk, salt, lemon extract and yeast mixture; mix well. Add flour; mix and knead well until a soft dough forms. Place dough in a greased bowl; cover with a tea towel and let rise in a warm place until double in size, about one hour. Roll out dough 1/2-inch thick; cut with a doughnut cutter. Let doughnuts rise, uncovered, about 30 minutes. In a deep saucepan, heat several inches of oil to 375 degrees. Fry doughnuts, a few at a time, until golden; drain. Sprinkle with cinnamon-sugar or powdered sugar.

★ VARIETY FOR FUN ★ Doughnut kabobs... a fun idea for a brunch buffet! Slide bite-size doughnuts onto wooden skewers and stand the skewers in a tall vase for easy serving.

Potato Doughnuts

Mary Jane Tolman, Rocky Mount, NC

Sweet Twists

These go great with a tall glass of cold milk for dunking.

Makes 2 dozen

1 env. active dry yeast
1/4 c. warm water
3-3/4 c. all-purpose flour
1-1/2 t. salt
1 c. butter
2 eggs, beaten
1/2 c. sour cream
3 t. vanilla extract, divided
1-1/2 c. sugar

Dissolve yeast in very warm water, 110 to 115 degrees; set aside. Mix flour and salt in a large bowl; cut in butter until coarse crumbs form. Blend in eggs, sour cream, one teaspoon vanilla and yeast mixture; cover and chill overnight. Combine sugar and remaining vanilla. Sprinkle 1/2 cup vanilla-sugar mixture on a flat surface; roll out dough into a 16-inch by 8-inch rectangle. Sprinkle one tablespoon of vanilla-sugar mixture over dough; fold dough over and roll into a rectangle again. Continue sprinkling mixture, folding and rolling until no vanilla-sugar remains. Cut dough into 4-inch by 1-inch strips; twist strips and place on greased baking sheets. Bake at 350 degrees for 15 to 20 minutes.

Selma Cherkas, Worcester, MA

Ginger & Currant Scones

The candied ginger adds a spicy sweetness to these scones that goes so well with the currants.

Makes 8 to 10 scones

1 egg, beaten
3 T. brown sugar, packed
1 t. rum or rum-flavored extract
1 t. baking powder
2 T. milk
1 c. all-purpose flour
1/4 c. butter, softened
3/4 c. currants
2 T. candied ginger, chopped

In a large bowl, mix together all ingredients until well blended. Divide dough into 8 to 10 balls; flatten. Arrange scones on ungreased baking sheets. Bake at 350 degrees for 15 minutes, or until golden.

★ FLAVOR BURST ★ **Dress up** homemade scones in a snap...drizzle with melted white chocolate or powdered sugar icing.

Sweet Twists

Dawn Menard, Seekonk, MA

Trudy's Cherry Coffee Cake

This was given to me by my friend Kelley...it's a recipe from her mother, Trudy. I like to make it with different fruit fillings, such as blueberry or apple, and various nuts, such as pecans or almonds. My son requests it often!

Serves 6 to 8

1-3/4 c. biscuit baking mix, divided
1 egg, beaten
1/2 c. sugar
1/4 c. milk
1/2 t. vanilla extract
1/8 t. salt
21-oz. can cherry pie filling, partially drained
1/2 c. brown sugar, packed
1/3 c. chopped walnuts
1/2 t. cinnamon
3 T. butter, diced

Combine 1-1/2 cups baking mix, egg, sugar, milk, vanilla and salt. Stir until smooth. Press mixture into a lightly greased 8"x8" baking pan. Spoon pie filling over mixture in pan. Mix together remaining baking mix, brown sugar, nuts, cinnamon and butter using a pastry blender or fork until crumbly. Sprinkle over pie filling. Bake at 375 degrees for 30 minutes. Cut into squares.

Violet Leonard, Chesapeake, VA

Morning Glory Muffins

These muffins are fantastic and filling. You can keep them in the freezer and thaw as needed.

Makes 1-1/2 dozen

2 c. all-purpose flour
1-1/4 c. sugar
2 t. baking soda
2 t. cinnamon
1/2 t. salt
2 c. carrots, peeled and grated
1/2 c. raisins
1/2 c. chopped pecans
3 eggs, beaten
1 c. oil
1 apple, peeled, cored and shredded
2 t. vanilla extract

In a large bowl, combine flour, sugar, baking soda, cinnamon and salt. Stir in carrots, raisins and pecans. In a separate bowl, combine eggs, oil, apple and vanilla. Add egg mixture to flour mixture; stir until just combined. Spoon into greased or paper-lined muffin cups, filling 3/4 full. Bake at 350 degrees for 15 to 18 minutes, until golden.

Trudy's Cherry Coffee Cake

Sandy Glennen, Dandridge, TN

Pecan Pie Muffins

Perfectly nutty and sweet! Oh-so-good with a cup of tea.

Makes 2-1/2 to 3 dozen

1 c. light brown sugar, packed
1/2 c. all-purpose flour
2 eggs, beaten
2/3 c. butter, melted
1 c. chopped pecans
Optional: pecan halves

In a bowl, stir together all ingredients except pecan halves. Fill greased mini muffin cups 2/3 full. Top each with a pecan half, if using. Bake at 350 degrees for 12 to 15 minutes, until golden.

Laura Carter, Vinita, OK

Overnight Caramel Pecan Rolls

I got this recipe from my grandmother and mother...it's a family favorite that we all enjoy.

Serves 10 to 12

2 3.4-oz. pkgs. instant
   butterscotch pudding mix
1 c. brown sugar, packed
1 c. chopped pecans
1/2 c. chilled butter
36 frozen rolls, divided

Combine dry pudding mixes, brown sugar and pecans in a bowl. Cut in butter; set aside. Arrange half the frozen rolls in a lightly greased Bundt® pan. Sprinkle half the pudding mixture over top. Repeat layering with remaining rolls and pudding mixture. Cover loosely; refrigerate overnight. Bake at 350 degrees for one hour. Invert onto a serving plate.

Pecan Pie Muffins

Vickie, Gooseberry Patch

Ginger Scones

Top these yummy scones with sweetened whipped cream!

Makes 8 scones

2-3/4 c. all-purpose flour
2 t. baking powder
1/2 t. salt
1/2 c. sugar
3/4 c. butter
1/3 c. crystallized ginger, chopped
1 c. milk

Combine first 4 ingredients in a large bowl; cut butter into flour mixture with a pastry blender until crumbly. Stir in ginger. Add milk, stirring just until dry ingredients are moistened. Turn dough out onto a lightly floured surface and knead 10 to 15 times. Pat or roll dough to 3/4-inch thickness; shape into a round and cut dough into 8 wedges. Place wedges on a lightly greased baking sheet. Bake at 400 degrees for 18 to 22 minutes, until scones are barely golden. Cool slightly on a wire rack.

Kathy Hanson, Knoxville, TN

Buttery Scones

Serve warm with butter, honey, jam and, of course, your favorite tea!

Makes one dozen

1 c. buttermilk
1 egg
2 to 3 T. sugar
3-1/2 c. unbleached white flour, divided
2 t. baking powder
1 t. baking soda
1/2 t. salt
1/2 c. butter, melted
1/2 c. raisins

Beat buttermilk, egg and sugar together with an electric mixer at medium speed. Sift 3 cups of flour with baking powder, baking soda and salt. Add 2/3 of the flour mixture to the buttermilk mixture and stir well. Gradually add melted butter, stirring well; add remaining flour mixture. Add raisins and a bit more flour if needed. Knead dough on a floured surface 2 to 3 times. Cut dough into 3 parts. Form each into a 1-1/2 inch thick circle and cut into 4 equal quarters. Place on a greased baking sheet. Bake at 400 degrees for 15 minutes, or until tops are golden.

Ginger Scones

Paige Woodard, Loveland, CO

Mocha Muffins

These taste great with or without the cream cheese spread. You can even top them with a bit of chocolate frosting if you like.

Makes 16 muffins

2 c. all-purpose flour
3/4 c. plus 1 T. sugar
2-1/2 t. baking powder
1 t. cinnamon
1/2 t. salt
1 c. milk
2 T. plus 1/2 t. instant coffee
    granules, divided
1/2 c. butter, melted
1 egg, beaten
1-1/2 t. vanilla extract, divided
1 c. mini semi-sweet chocolate
    chips, divided
1/2 c. cream cheese, softened

Whisk together flour, sugar, baking powder, cinnamon and salt in a large bowl. Stir together milk and 2 tablespoons coffee granules in a separate bowl until coffee is dissolved. Add butter, egg and one teaspoon vanilla; mix well. Stir into dry ingredients until just moistened. Fold in 3/4 cup chocolate chips. Fill greased or paper-lined muffin cups 2/3 full. Bake at 375 degrees for 17 to 20 minutes. Cool for 5 minutes before removing from pans to wire racks. Combine cream cheese and remaining coffee granules, vanilla and chocolate chips in a food processor or blender. Cover and process until well blended. Refrigerate spread until serving time. Serve spread on side.

★ DOUBLE DUTY ★ Have a bit of this mocha cream cheese spread left over? Try it with sliced apples or pears for an afternoon treat!

Mocha Muffins

Maria Temple, New York, NY

Sugar-Topped Muffins

Enjoy these warm muffins for
a real treat!

Makes 2 dozen

18-1/4 oz. pkg. white cake mix
1 c. milk
2 eggs, beaten
1/2 t. nutmeg
1/3 c. sugar
1/2 t. cinnamon
1/4 c. butter, melted

Beat cake mix, milk, eggs and nutmeg at low speed with an electric mixer until just moistened; beat at high speed 2 minutes. Fill paper-lined muffin cups 2/3 full. Bake at 350 degrees until golden, about 15 to 18 minutes. Cool 5 minutes. Combine sugar and cinnamon on a small plate. Brush muffin tops with butter; roll in sugar and cinnamon mixture. Serve warm.

★ VARIETY FOR FUN ★ Keep a few different flavors of cake mix and pie filling on hand...mix & match to make lots of delicious muffins, cupcakes and cobblers for potlucks or entertaining friends.

Sugar-Topped Muffins

Joyceann Dreibelbis, Wooster, OH

Cherry Streusel Coffee Cake

This easy-to-assemble coffee cake recipe won "Best of Show" several years ago at a county fair, and it's been requested at many social events.

Makes 15 servings

16-1/2 oz. pkg. yellow cake mix, divided
1 env. active dry yeast
1 c. all-purpose flour
2 eggs, beaten
2/3 c. warm water
5 T. butter, melted
21-oz. can cherry pie filling
2 T. sugar
Optional: chopped nuts

Combine 1-1/2 cups dry cake mix, yeast, flour, eggs and warm water (110 to 115 degrees); stir for 2 minutes. Spread in a lightly greased 13"x9" baking pan. Blend melted butter and remaining cake mix; set aside. Spoon pie filling over batter in pan. Crumble butter mixture over pie filling. Sprinkle sugar over top. Bake at 375 degrees for 30 minutes. Let cool. Drizzle Glaze over cooled cake; sprinkle nuts on top, if desired.

Glaze:

1 c. powdered sugar
1 T. corn syrup
1 to 2 T. water

Combine powdered sugar and corn syrup. Stir in enough water to form a glaze consistency.

★ HOT TIP ★ Serve hot spiced coffee with fresh-baked coffee cake. Simply add 3/4 teaspoon apple pie spice to 1/2 cup ground coffee and brew as usual.

Cherry Streusel Coffee Cake

Barbara Girlardo, Pittsburgh, PA

Cranberry Upside-Down Muffins

Served warm, these tangy muffins are delicious alongside breakfast dishes... soups and stews too!

Makes 1-1/2 dozen

2- 1/2 c. all-purpose flour
1/2 c. sugar
1 T. baking powder
1/2 t. salt
1-1/4 c. milk
1/3 c. butter, melted and slightly
 cooled
1 egg, beaten

Combine flour, sugar, baking powder and salt in a large bowl; blend well. Add milk, butter and egg to flour mixture; stir just until moistened. Spoon Cranberry Topping into 18 greased muffin cups. Spoon batter over topping, filling each cup 2/3 full. Bake at 400 degrees for 16 to 18 minutes, until a toothpick inserted in center comes out clean. Immediately invert onto a wire rack placed on wax paper; serve warm.

Cranberry Topping:

1/2 c. cranberries, halved
1/2 c. chopped nuts
1/3 c. brown sugar, packed
1/4 c. butter
1/2 t. cinnamon

Combine all ingredients in a small saucepan. Cook over medium heat until brown sugar dissolves. Cool 10 minutes.

★ FREEZE IT ★ Stock up on fresh cranberries when they're available every autumn to add their fruity tang to cookies, quick breads and sauces year 'round. Simply pop unopened bags in the freezer.

Cranberry Upside-Down Muffins

Carol Courter, Delaware, OH

Jumbo Cinnamon Rolls

Mmm...treat the whole family to these scrumptious, ooey-gooey warm rolls!

Makes one dozen

1 c. very warm milk (110 degrees)
1 env. active dry yeast
1/2 c. sugar
2 eggs, beaten
1/3 c. margarine, melted and cooled
1 t. salt
4-1/2 c. all-purpose flour
3/4 c. brown sugar, packed
1/3 c. butter, softened
2-1/2 T. cinnamon
16-oz. container cream cheese
   frosting

Combine milk, yeast and sugar in a large bowl; let stand for 10 minutes. Stir in eggs and margarine with a wooden spoon. Mix salt into flour; add flour to milk mixture one cup at a time until dough forms. Knead until smooth; place dough in a large bowl sprayed with non-stick vegetable spray. Cover; let rest until double in size. Generously spray a surface with non-stick vegetable spray; roll out dough into a 21-inch by 16-inch rectangle. Spread with butter; combine brown sugar and cinnamon and sprinkle over top. Roll up dough and slice into 12 rolls; arrange in a lightly greased 13"x9" baking pan. Cover and let rise until nearly double in size, about 30 minutes. Bake at 400 degrees until golden, about 15 minutes. Spread warm rolls with frosting; serve warm.

Debi Gilpin, Bluefield, WV

Twisty Rolls

I have been making these for years...but my dear Aunt Betty will always be the undisputed world champion Twisty Roll maker!

Makes 14 rolls

1 env. active dry yeast
3 T. sugar, divided
1/4 c. warm water
1-1/2 t. salt
4-1/4 c. all-purpose flour, divided
1/4 c. butter, melted and cooled
3/4 c. milk plus 2 T. milk, divided
2 eggs, divided
1 T. water
1 c. powdered sugar
2 T. milk

Dissolve yeast and one teaspoon sugar in warm water (110 to 115 degrees); set aside. Mix remaining sugar, salt and 2 cups flour. Add yeast mixture, melted butter and 3/4 cup milk. Stir until smooth. Beat in one egg. Add enough flour to make a soft dough. Knead in remaining flour until dough is smooth and elastic (about 5 minutes). Place in greased bowl, cover and let rise in a warm place (85 degrees), away from drafts, until doubled, about 40 minutes. Punch down and roll out to a 1/4-inch thickness on a floured surface. Cut into 6-inch by 1/2-inch strips; braid 3 strips together to form a roll. Combine one tablespoon water and remaining egg. Place braids on a baking sheet and brush with egg mixture. Let rise 15 to 20 more minutes. Bake at 375 degrees for 10 to 12 minutes. Let cool. Blend together powdered sugar and milk; drizzle over cooled rolls.

Jumbo Cinnamon Rolls

Donna Grove, Saint Petersburg, FL

Double Toffee Coffee Cake

Just right for sharing with special friends.

Serves 8 to 10

1/2 c. brown sugar, packed
1 c. pecans, finely chopped
1 T. cinnamon
2 c. all-purpose flour
3.4-oz. pkg. instant vanilla pudding mix
3.4-oz. pkg. instant butterscotch pudding mix
1 c. sugar
2 t. baking powder
1 t. salt
1 c. water
3/4 c. oil
1 t. vanilla extract
4 eggs, beaten

Combine brown sugar, pecans and cinnamon in a small bowl; set aside. Combine remaining ingredients in a large bowl; beat for 2 minutes with an electric mixer on medium speed. Pour a little less than half the batter into a greased 13"x9" baking pan; sprinkle with half the brown sugar mixture. Pour remaining batter on top; sprinkle with remaining brown sugar mixture. Bake at 350 degrees for 40 to 45 minutes.

Robin Long, Newberry, SC

Cream Cheese Danish

Did you get out of bed on the wrong side today? You'll feel so much better after you've tasted this!

Serves 15 to 20

2 8-oz. pkgs. cream cheese, softened
3/4 c. sugar
1 egg yolk, beaten
2 t. lemon juice
1 t. vanilla extract
2 8-oz. tubes refrigerated crescent rolls
2 c. powdered sugar
4 to 5 T. milk

Blend together cream cheese and sugar in a large bowl; add egg yolk, lemon juice and vanilla. Set aside. Layer one tube of crescent rolls in bottom of a greased 13"x9" baking pan; press seams together. Spread cream cheese mixture over top; layer remaining tube of rolls on top of cream cheese. Bake at 350 degrees for 15 to 20 minutes, until golden. Let cool. Mix together powdered sugar and milk to a thin consistency; drizzle over top. Cut into slices to serve.

Double Toffee Coffee Cake

Wendy Lee Paffenroth, Pine Island, NY

Pumpkin Biscotti

Slices of biscotti are so nice to give to a co-worker along with a tea bag... a welcome morning treat. Try a gingerbread muffin or quick bread mix, too...scrumptious!

Serves 6 to 8

4 eggs, beaten
1 c. butter, melted and slightly cooled
1 t. vanilla extract
2 14-oz. pkgs. pumpkin muffin or
    quick bread mix
12-oz. white or milk chocolate chips,
    divided
1 to 3 T. all-purpose flour

Combine eggs, butter and vanilla in a large bowl; stir until well blended. Blend in dry muffin or quick bread mix and 1/2 cup chocolate chips; stir again. Mixture will be sticky. Add enough flour to form a smooth dough; knead on a lightly floured surface for several minutes. Divide dough in half; shape each half into an oval loaf and flatten slightly. Place on a lightly greased baking sheet and bake at 350 degrees for 30 to 40 minutes, until golden. Remove from oven and set aside to cool 15 to 20 minutes. Cut loaves into one-inch thick slices with a serrated knife; arrange on baking sheet. Return to oven and continue to bake 15 more minutes. Remove from oven and set aside to cool. Melt remaining chocolate chips and drizzle over slices; cool.

★ GIFT IT ★ Wrap several biscotti in festive cellophane and tie with curling ribbons to a package of gourmet coffee beans...a coffee lover's delight!

Pumpkin Biscotti

Jeanne Barringer, Edgewater, FL

Sour Cream Mini Biscuits

This recipe makes several dozen bite-size biscuits...ideal for filling gift baskets or taking to a potluck.

Makes 4 dozen

1 c. butter, softened
1 c. sour cream
2 c. self-rising flour

Blend butter and sour cream together until fluffy; gradually mix in flour. Drop teaspoonfuls of dough into greased mini muffin cups; bake at 450 degrees for 10 to 12 minutes.

Tracey Graham, Churubusco, IN

Supreme Caramel Apple Rolls

This is one of my family's most-requested recipes. One time after serving them, one of my seven brothers told me, "These rolls are so bad, I need to take the rest home with me to eat!

Makes 2 dozen rolls

21-oz. can apple pie filling
1/2 c. caramel ice cream topping
Optional: 1/2 c. chopped pecans
8-oz. pkg. cream cheese, softened
1/3 c. powdered sugar
2 8-oz. tubes refrigerated crescent
   rolls
1/2 c. sugar
1/2 c. brown sugar, packed
1/2 c. butter, melted

Combine pie filling and ice cream topping in a large bowl; pour into a greased 13"x9" baking pan. Sprinkle pecans, if using, over mixture. Combine cream cheese and powdered sugar in a bowl; set aside. Separate crescent roll dough into 2 rectangles; press perforations to seal. Spread half of cream cheese mixture over each rectangle. Starting with long side of each rectangle, roll up and seal edges. Cut each roll into 12 slices with a serrated knife. Stir together sugar and brown sugar in a bowl; dip slices in melted butter and then coat with sugar mixture. Arrange slices in baking pan. Bake at 400 degrees for 25 to 30 minutes, until center rolls are golden. Immediately invert onto a serving plate. Serve warm.

Sour Cream Mini Biscuits

Katie Majeske, Denver, PA

Mom's Orange Bow Knots

I still love going home to find these amazing rolls in Mom's kitchen! The recipe goes back a few generations in my family. Quick breads may be easier, but nothing tastes better than yeast bread.

Makes 2 to 3 dozen

1-1/4 c. milk
1/2 c. shortening
1/3 c. sugar
3/4 t. salt
1 env. active dry yeast
2 eggs, beaten
1/4 c. orange juice
2 T. orange zest
5 c. all-purpose flour, divided

Heat milk just to boiling. Combine milk, shortening, sugar and salt in a bowl; let cool to about 110 to 115 degrees. Dissolve yeast in milk mixture. Add eggs, orange juice and orange zest; beat well. Stir in 2 cups flour; let stand 10 minutes. Stir in remaining flour. Cover with a tea towel; let rise until doubled, one to 2 hours. Punch down dough; roll out 1/2-inch thick on a floured surface. Cut into 10-inch by 1/2-inch strips. Tie each strip loosely in a bow; arrange on lightly greased baking sheets. Cover and let rise again, 30 minutes to one hour. Bake at 375 degrees for 15 minutes, or until golden. Cool; spread with Orange Frosting.

Orange Frosting:

1 c. powdered sugar
2 T. orange juice
1 t. orange zest

Stir together all ingredients, adding powdered sugar to desired consistency.

★ GIFT IT ★ Bake homemade yeast sweet rolls and deliver to friends and neighbors on Christmas Eve day, in time to eat on Christmas morning. What a treat!

Mom's Orange Bow Knots

Frosty Lime-Mint Tea, Page 240

CHAPTER SEVEN

Beverages

Malted Hot Cocoa, Page 236

Icy Raspberry Tea, Page 246

Beth Bundy, Long Prairie, MN

Cheery Cherry Punch

The sweet-tart flavors of cherry, apple, pineapple and lemon combine in this fruity concoction...along with a fizzy splash of ginger ale.

Makes 3 quarts

3-oz. pkg. cherry gelatin mix
1 c. hot water
46-oz. can pineapple juice, chilled
4 c. apple juice, chilled
3/4 c. lemon juice
1 ltr. ginger ale, chilled
Garnishes: maraschino cherries,
   lemon wedges

Stir together gelatin mix and hot water in a small bowl until gelatin dissolves. Pour into a large pitcher, stir in juices; chill. When ready to serve, add ginger ale to pitcher, gently stirring to combine.

Jennie Gist, Gooseberry Patch

Green Tea Limeade

Refreshing and not too sweet!

Makes 20 servings

2 c. boiling water
4 green tea bags
2 12-oz. cans frozen limeade
   concentrate
Garnish: lime wedges

In a teapot, combine boiling water and tea bags. Let stand for 10 minutes. Discard tea bags; let tea cool slightly. In a large pitcher, prepare frozen limeade according to package directions. Stir in tea; cover and chill. Garnish with lime wedges.

★ DOUBLE DUTY ★ Be sure to save the red juice from jars of maraschino cherries. Stir a little of it into punch, lemonade, ginger ale or milk for a sweet pink drink that kids will love.

Cheery Cherry Punch

Jennifer Niemi,

Nova Scotia. Canada

Hot Lemon Spice Tea

This tea really takes the chill off on a cold winter's day.

Makes 12 servings

zest of one lemon
4-inch cinnamon stick
1-1/2 inch slice fresh ginger,
    peeled and thinly sliced
12 c. water, divided
1 c. instant tea mix
1/2 c. lemonade drink mix

Combine zest, cinnamon stick, ginger and 2 cups water in a large saucepan. Bring to a boil over medium heat. Reduce heat, cover and simmer for 15 minutes. Strain and discard spices. In a large pot, combine remaining water, tea mix and lemonade mix; stir in strained mixture. Cook over low heat, stirring often, until sugar is dissolved. Increase heat to medium-high; heat until piping hot.

April Garner, Independence, KY

Cinnamon Ice Cubes

This is a family favorite from Thanksgiving to New Year's Eve. Serve them in tall glasses of iced tea or soda.

Makes 4 to 5 dozen

1/2 c. red cinnamon candies
1/2 c. water
3 c. orange juice

Combine candies and water in a medium saucepan over medium heat. Bring to a boil; simmer, stirring constantly, until candies are dissolved. Add orange juice; mix well. Pour into ice cube trays; freeze.

★ FREEZE IT ★ Want to make big, colorful ice cubes for a party punch bowl? Arrange fresh cranberries or thin slices of citrus in muffin tins, fill with water and freeze.

Hot Lemon Spice Tea

Amy Butcher, Columbus, GA

Old-Fashioned Ginger Beer

So refreshing any time of year!

Serves 8 to 10

4 lemons
1 orange
3/4 c. fresh ginger, peeled and
  coarsely chopped
3/4 c. sugar
3/4 c. honey
2 c. boiling water
1-1/4 c. orange juice
4 c. sparkling mineral water, chilled
crushed ice
Garnish: orange slices

Grate 2 tablespoons of zest from lemons and orange. Set orange and one lemon aside. Squeeze 1/3 cup lemon juice from remaining 3 lemons. Set aside. Pulse ginger, sugar and honey in a food processor just until combined; spoon into a pitcher. Add orange and lemon zests and boiling water; stir until sugar dissolves. Cool to room temperature. Stir in orange juice. Cover and refrigerate for at least 24 hours and up to 5 days. Strain before serving. Thinly slice remaining lemon and orange; add to pitcher. Stir in sparkling water. Serve over ice. Garnish, as desired.

★ FLAVOR BURST ★ Dress up plain orange juice in a jiffy! Add a spash of fizzy ginger ale and serve it up in stemmed glasses trimmed with ribbon bows... an oh-so-simple touch that guests will remember.

Old-Fashioned Ginger Beer

Regina Vining, Warwick, RI

Spiced Chocolate Coffee

This sweet sipper is conveniently made in a slow cooker. Top with sweetened whipped cream for a special treat.

Makes about 8 cups

8 c. brewed coffee
1/3 c. sugar
1/4 c. chocolate syrup
4 4-inch cinnamon sticks, broken
1-1/2 t. whole cloves
Garnish: cinnamon sticks, sweetened
    whipped cream

Combine first 3 ingredients in a 3-quart slow cooker; set aside. Wrap spices in a coffee filter or cheesecloth and tie with kitchen string; add to slow cooker. Cover and cook on low setting for 2 to 3 hours. Remove and discard spices. Ladle coffee into mugs and garnish.

Loni Ventura, Wimauma, FL

Warm Spiced Milk

A tummy-warming beverage... tastes like a baked apple in a mug!

Makes 4 servings

2-1/2 c. milk
1/3 c. apple butter
2-1/2 T. maple syrup
1/4 t. cinnamon
1/8 t. ground cloves

Whisk ingredients together in a heavy saucepan. Heat over low heat until milk steams; do not boil.

★ KID FRIENDLY ★ A little "magic" for the kids! Put a drop of green food coloring into their milk glasses, then fill with milk as you tap the glasses with a magic wand.

Spiced Chocolate Coffee

Brenda Smith, Delaware, OH

Honeyed Fruit Juice

Coming in from ice skating, we were chilled to the bone. Luckily Mom had this wonderful juice blend warming in the slow cooker!

Makes 3 quarts

64-oz. bottle cranberry-apple juice
   cocktail
2 c. apple juice
1 c. pomegranate juice
1/2 c. orange juice
2/3 c. honey
3 4-inch cinnamon sticks
10 whole cloves
2 T. orange zest

Combine juices and honey in a slow cooker. Wrap cinnamon sticks and cloves in a double thickness of cheesecloth; bring up corners of cloth and tie with kitchen string to form a bag. Add to slow cooker along with zest. Cover and cook on low setting for one to 2 hours. Discard spice bag before serving.

Kim Warren, Hodgenville, KY

Lemon-Berry Sparkler

We've been cutting back on regular soda, so I've come up with several homemade, healthier versions. So refreshing!

Makes 6 servings

1 c. frozen blackberries, thawed
   and divided
1 c. frozen raspberries, thawed and
   divided
1/2 c. sugar
3-1/2 c. water, divided
1/3 c. lemonade drink mix
ice cubes
seltzer water or club soda, chilled

Return a few berries to the freezer for garnish. With a potato masher, mash remaining berries with sugar in a large bowl. Stir in 1/2 cup water; let stand for 10 minutes. Strain berry mixture through a fine strainer over a pitcher. Add drink mix and remaining water to pitcher; stir to combine. Chill. To serve, fill glasses 1/2 full of ice and add a few reserved frozen berries. Fill glasses 2/3 full with berry mixture; top off with seltzer water or club soda. Stir and serve.

Honeyed Fruit Juice

Geneva Rogers, Gillette, WY

White Hot Chocolate

Serve in thick mugs with whipped cream, a dash of cinnamon or cocoa powder and a candy cane.

Makes 3 cups

3 c. half-and-half, divided
2/3 c. white chocolate chips
3-inch cinnamon stick
1/8 t. nutmeg
1 t. vanilla extract
1/4 t. almond extract
Garnish: whipped topping, cinnamon
 and candy canes

In a saucepan, combine 1/4 cup half-and-half, white chocolate chips, cinnamon stick and nutmeg. Whisk over low heat until chips are melted. Remove cinnamon stick. Add remaining half-and-half. Whisk until heated throughout. Remove from heat and add vanilla and almond extracts. Garnish with whipped topping, cinnamon and candy canes.

★ VARIETY FOR FUN ★ Host a dessert open house for friends & neighbors instead of an elaborate holiday party. Serve lots of cookies with coffee, tea and festive mulled cider or hot cocoa...just add fun and fellowship for a delightful no-stress afternoon!

White Hot Chocolate

Jill Burton, Gooseberry Patch

Iced Vanilla Caramel Coffee

This is a real treat!

Makes 4 servings

4 c. brewed coffee
1 c. milk
1/3 c. non-dairy vanilla coffee
   creamer
1/4 c. caramel ice cream topping
3 c. crushed ice
Optional: whipped cream

In a blender, combine all ingredients except whipped cream. Process on high until completely smooth. Pour into 4 glasses; garnish with whipped cream, if desired.

Geneva Rogers, Gillette, WY

Splendid Mocha Coffee

I was recently diagnosed with diabetes, so I had to give up a lot of my favorite sweet treats. This coffee is so yummy, it's hard to believe it isn't loaded with real sugar. For an extra-special indulgence, sometimes I add a dollop of sugar-free whipped topping and a dusting of cocoa.

Makes one serving

1 c. hot brewed coffee
1 t. baking cocoa
2 T. fat-free milk
1 t. calorie-free powdered
   sweetener for coffee

Pour hot coffee into a warmed mug. Stir in cocoa, milk and sweetener until well blended. Serve immediately...enjoy!

★ HOT TIP ★ Make coffee-shop style drinks at home...personalize them! Fill a pastry bag with melted caramel and drizzle designs on wax paper...try hearts, stars and friends' initials. Freeze caramel until firm, then use to top each beverage.

Iced Vanilla Caramel Coffee

JoAnna Brown, Ann Arbor, MI

Malted Hot Cocoa

A hot, creamy beverage that's just a little different.

Makes 4 servings

6 1-oz. sqs. bittersweet baking chocolate, chopped
1/2 c. boiling water
1/2 c. whipping cream
1 c. milk
3 T. malted milk powder
Garnish: whipped topping, crushed malted milk ball candies

Place chocolate in a small bowl; pour boiling water over chocolate. Let stand for 3 minutes. In a small saucepan, combine cream and milk over medium heat; bring to a simmer. Stir in malted milk powder; set aside. Whisk chocolate mixture until smooth; add to milk mixture. Garnish with whipped topping and crushed candies.

★ SKINNY SECRET ★ Bittersweet baking chocolate contains less sugar than semi-sweet and is called for in recipes that are looking for deep, intense chocolate flavor. Semi-sweet chocolate can usually be substituted with good success.

Malted Hot Cocoa

Della Feist, Faith, SD

Cranberry-Orange Warmer

This is a favorite drink around our home during the fall and winter holidays. Make a double batch and invite friends over.

Makes 20 servings

16-oz. pkg. frozen cranberries, thawed
4-inch cinnamon stick
8 c. water
6-oz. can frozen orange juice concentrate, thawed
6-oz. can frozen lemonade concentrate, thawed
1 c. sugar

In a saucepan, bring cranberries, cinnamon stick and water to a boil. Boil for 5 minutes. Strain, discarding cranberries and cinnamon stick. Return juice to saucepan. Add juice concentrates and sugar to saucepan; stir until sugar dissolves. Serve warm.

Liz Plotnick-Snay, Gooseberry Patch

Hot Tomato Cocktail

A zippy beverage just right for chilly nights at the football stadium.

Makes 6 to 8 servings

46-oz. can cocktail vegetable juice
2 T. brown sugar, packed
2 T. lemon juice
1-1/2 t. prepared horseradish
1 t. Worcestershire sauce
1/4 t. hot pepper sauce
1 stalk celery, cut into 3 pieces

Combine all ingredients in a 3-quart slow cooker; stir. Cover and cook on low setting for 3 to 4 hours. Discard celery; serve hot.

★ DOUBLE DUTY ★ For a warm, cozy holiday fragrance, simmer cinnamon sticks, citrus peel, whole cloves and nutmeg in a mini slow cooker. Just add 2 to 3 cups of water and set on low.

Cranberry-Orange Warmer

Sara Richards, Tucson, AZ

Frosty Lime-Mint Tea

I've made this tea with lemons too. It's just as refreshing!

Serves 10 to 12

4 c. brewed tea
1-1/2 c. sugar, or to taste
10 to 12 c. water
juice of 6 limes
8 to 10 fresh mint sprigs
Optional: additional mint, fresh
   raspberries

Combine brewed tea and sugar in a one-gallon pitcher. Stir in enough water to equal one gallon. Add lime juice and mint sprigs; stir until sugar is dissolved. Cover and chill. Serve over ice, garnished as desired.

Jill Valentine, Jackson, TN

Warm Spiced Apricot Punch

The spicy scent will welcome everyone to breakfast.

Makes 6 servings

2 12-oz. cans apricot nectar
2 c. water
1/4 c. lemon juice
1/4 c. sugar
6 whole cloves
2 4-inch cinnamon sticks

Combine all ingredients in a slow cooker; mix well. Cover and cook on low setting for 2 hours. Strain to remove spices before serving.

★ SAVVY SWAP ★ Out of apricot nectar for a recipe? Peach or pear juice work just as well and taste delicious.

Frosty Lime-Mint Tea

Mary Murray, Mt. Vernon, OH

Refreshing Mint Punch

With only four ingredients, this crowd-pleasing punch is easy to mix up.

Serves 10 to 12

2 c. fresh mint leaves, packed
2 c. water
12-oz. can frozen lemonade
   concentrate, thawed
1 qt. ginger ale

Bring mint and water to boil; bruise mint with potato masher. Set aside overnight; strain and discard solids. Add lemonade, 3 lemonade cans of water and ginger ale to mint mixture; mix well and serve.

Julie Harris, Boiling Springs, SC

Yankee Iced Tea

Growing up in the Pennsylvania countryside, I remember my mom making this tea for my dad every evening to go alongside one of her hearty homemade dinners. Following in my mom's footsteps, I now make this often for my own husband. Add a full cup of sugar if you like your tea sweeter.

Makes 4 to 6 servings

2 c. boiling water
6 tea bags
1/8 t. baking soda
3/4 c. sugar
6 c. cold water
Garnish: ice cubes, lemon wedges

In a one-gallon pitcher, combine boiling water and tea bags. Cover; let stand for 15 to 20 minutes to steep. Remove tea bags. Stir in baking soda and sugar until dissolved. Add cold water; cover and refrigerate. Serve over ice cubes with a squeeze of lemon.

★ VARIETY FOR FUN ★ Add a little flair to your party punch! Scoop a quart of lemon or raspberry sherbet into 8 balls and freeze until serving time. To serve, place each ball in a frosted stemmed glass. Carefully pour 1/2 cup chilled punch over the sherbet and garnish with a sprig of fresh mint.

Refreshing Mint Punch

Debi DeVore, Dover, OH

Maple Hot Chocolate

Chocolatey made-from-scratch hot cocoa...even yummier with a little maple flavoring stirred in!

Makes 4 servings

1/4 c. sugar
1 T. baking cocoa
1/8 t. salt
1/4 c. hot water
1 T. butter
4 c. milk
1 t. maple flavoring
1 t. vanilla extract
12 marshmallows, divided

Combine sugar, cocoa and salt in a large saucepan. Stir in hot water and butter; bring to a boil over medium heat. Add milk, maple flavoring, vanilla and 8 marshmallows. Heat through, stirring occasionally, until marshmallows are melted. Ladle into 4 mugs; top with remaining marshmallows.

Tiffany Brinkley, Broomfield, CO

Buttermint Coffee Creamer

For a fun gift, pack in mini jars... wrap some more mints in circles of tulle and tie onto jars for nibbling.

Makes about 5 cups

7-oz. pkg. buttermints, crushed
2 c. powdered non-dairy coffee creamer
2 c. chocolate malt powder
1/2 c. chocolate drink mix

Combine all ingredients in a blender. Process at high spend until well blended. Store in an airtight container.

★ VARIETY FOR FUN ★ Set up a coffee station for friends to enjoy while nibbling on dessert. Make it extra special by offering flavored creamers, candied stirrers and scrumptious toppings like whipped cream, cinnamon and chocolate shavings.

Maple Hot Chocolate

Trisha Brady, Belmont, MA

Icy Raspberry Tea

I make this for all of our family cook-outs. My kids love it!

Serves 6 to 8

4 c. brewed tea
3/4 c. sugar
16-oz. pkg. fresh or frozen
   raspberries
4 c. water
ice cubes

Add brewed tea to a large pitcher; stir in sugar and set aside. Combine raspberries and water in a large saucepan over medium heat; bring to a boil. Cook, stirring occasionally, for 5 minutes; remove from heat. Pour mixture through a strainer into a bowl, using the back of a spoon to press out the juice. Stir raspberry juice into tea mixture, discarding raspberry solids. Cover and chill for one hour. Serve over ice.

Molly Bordonaro, Worthington, OH

Frosty Orange Creamsicle

So cool and refreshing!

Makes 6 servings

6-oz. can frozen orange juice
   concentrate
1 c. milk
1 c. water
1 c. ice cubes
1/4 c. sugar
1/2 t. vanilla extract

Combine all ingredients in a blender until smooth. Serve immediately or freeze until ready to serve.

★ FREEZE IT ★ For a fruit-studded ice ring that won't dilute your party punch, arrange sliced oranges, lemons and limes in a ring mold. Pour in a small amount of punch and freeze until set. Add enough punch to fill mold and freeze until solid. To turn out, dip mold carefully in warm water.

Icy Raspberry Tea

Valarie Dennard, Palatka, FL

Chocolate Eggnog

A great no-fuss recipe for jazzing up store-bought eggnog.

Makes 3 quarts

2 qts. eggnog
16-oz. can chocolate syrup
Optional: 1/2 c. light rum
1 c. whipping cream
2 T. powdered sugar
Garnish: baking cocoa

Combine eggnog, chocolate syrup and rum, if using, in a punch bowl, stirring well. Beat whipping cream with an electric mixer on high speed until foamy. Add powdered sugar; continue beating until stiff peaks form. Dollop whipped cream over eggnog; sift cocoa over top. Serve immediately.

Linda Behling, Cecil, PA

Chai Tea

Typically a sweet tea...reduce the sugar even more if you'd like.

Serves 8 to 10

8 c. water
8 tea bags
1/2 to 3/4 c. sugar
16 whole cloves
5 4-inch cinnamon sticks
8 1-inch slices fresh ginger, peeled
Optional: 16 whole cardamom, seeds
   removed and pods discarded
1 c. milk

Combine all ingredients except milk in a slow cooker. Cover; cook on high setting for 2 to 2-1/2 hours. Strain and discard spices. Cover and refrigerate for up to 3 days, or serve immediately. Stir in milk just before serving. May be served warm or chilled.

★ TIME-SAVING SHORTCUT ★ For a terrific eggnog punch in a jiffy, combine one quart eggnog, 2 pints softened peppermint ice cream and one cup ginger ale. Delicious and easy to double for a crowd.

Chocolate Eggnog

Carrie O'Shea, Marina Del Rey, CA

Kitchen Café Mocha

Oh, café mocha is such a treat! I make this every Saturday to tote with me on errands.

Makes 6 servings

6 c. hot brewed coffee
3/4 c. half-and-half
6 T. chocolate syrup
2 T. plus 1 t. sugar
Garnish: whipped cream, chocolate
　syrup

In a large saucepan, combine all ingredients except garnish. Cook and stir over medium heat until sugar is dissolved and mixture is heated through. Pour into mugs and garnish as desired.

Jennie Gist, Gooseberry Patch

Ruby Red Tea Punch

Easy to make, not too sweet, a beautiful red color...what more could you ask for?

Makes 8 servings

4 c. boiling water
4 lemon hibiscus tea bags
4 raspberry hibiscus tea bags
4 c. apple juice
ice cubes

In a heatproof pitcher, combine boiling water and tea bags. Let stand for 10 minutes; discard tea bags. Stir in apple juice. Cover and chill. Serve over ice.

★ FLAVOR BURST ★ A cup of herbal tea is perfect with breakfast recipes. Instead of sweetening a cup of tea with sugar, drop in one or 2 old-fashioned lemon drops.

Kitchen Café Mocha

Index

Breakfast Mains

Breakfast Sandwiches

Breakfast Sides

Oatmeal, Granola & Cereal

Pancakes, Waffles & French Toast

Syrups

U. S. to Metric Recipe Equivalents

Volume Measurements

¼ teaspoon . . . . 1 mL
½ teaspoon . . . . 2 mL
1 teaspoon . . . . 5 mL
1 tablespoon = 3 teaspoons . . . . 15 mL
2 tablespoons = 1 fluid ounce . . . . 30 mL
¼ cup . . . . 60 mL
⅓ cup . . . . 75 mL
½ cup = 4 fluid ounces . . . . 125 mL
1 cup = 8 fluid ounces . . . . 250 mL
2 cups = 1 pint = 16 fluid ounces . . 500 mL
4 cups = 1 quart . . . . 1 L

Weights

1 ounce . . . . 30 g
4 ounces . . . . 120 g
8 ounces . . . . 225 g
16 ounces = 1 pound . . . . 450 g

Baking Pan Sizes

Square
8x8x2 inches . . . . 2 L = 20x20x5 cm
9x9x2 inches . . . . 2.5 L = 23x23x5 cm

Rectangular
13x9x2 inches . . . . 3.5 L = 33x23x5 cm

Loaf
9x5x3 inches . . . . 2 L = 23x13x7 cm

Round
8x1-1/2 inches . . . . 1.2 L = 20x4 cm
9x1-1/2 inches . . . . 1.5 L = 23x4 cm

Recipe Abbreviations

t. = teaspoon	ltr. = liter
T. = tablespoon	oz. = ounce
c. = cup	lb. = pound
pt. = pint	doz. = dozen
qt. = quart	pkg. = package
gal. = gallon	env. = envelope

Oven Temperatures

300˚ F . . . . 150° C
325˚ F . . . . 160° C
350˚ F . . . . 180° C
375˚ F . . . . 190° C
400˚ F . . . . 200° C
450˚ F . . . . 230° C

Kitchen Measurements

A pinch = ⅛ tablespoon
1 fluid ounce = 2 tablespoons
3 teaspoons = 1 tablespoon
4 fluid ounces = ½ cup
2 tablespoons = ⅛ cup
8 fluid ounces = 1 cup
4 tablespoons = ¼ cup
16 fluid ounces = 1 pint
8 tablespoons = ½ cup
32 fluid ounces = 1 quart
16 tablespoons = 1 cup
16 ounces net weight = 1 pound
2 cups = 1 pint
4 cups = 1 quart
4 quarts = 1 gallon